THE
LONG
ROAD
BACK

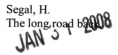

ALSO BY HUGH SEGAL

Geopolitical Integrity (editor)

In Defence of Civility: Reflections of a Recovering Politician

Beyond Greed: A Traditional Conservative Confronts Neo-conservative Excess

No Surrender: Reflections of a Happy Warrior in the Tory Crusade

Election: The Issues, the Strategies, the Aftermath (co-author)

No Small Measure: The Conservatives and the Constitution (co-author)

THE
LONG
ROAD
BACK

Creating Canada's
New Conservative Party

HUGH SEGAL

HarperCollins*PublishersLtd*

Published by HarperCollins Publishers Ltd.

Originally published in hardcover by HarperCollins Publishers Ltd: 2006
This trade paperback edition: 2007

HarperCollins books may be purchased for
educational, business, or sales promotional
use through our Special Markets Department.

HarperCollins Publishers Ltd
2 Bloor Street East, 20th Floor
Toronto, Ontario, Canada
M4W 1A8

www.harpercollins.ca

Library and Archives Canada Cataloguing in Publication is available

Segal, Hugh
The long road back: creating canada's new conservative party
Hugh Segal.—1st trade pbk ed.

ISBN-13: 978-0-00-200012-3
ISBN-10: 0-00-200012-1

RRD 1 2 3 4 5 6 7 8 9

Design by Sharon Kish
Printed and bound in the United States

For Donna,
without whose forbearance, advice,
perspective, and love over more than three decades
the road would have been too steep to travel.

Contents

INTRODUCTION

This book explores the history and prospects of the post–Cold War conservative cause in Canada. It follows the journey of the conservative movement in Canada over its decade-plus in the wilderness of factionalism, incompetence, and irrelevance back to its return to power in 2006. I began to write this book in 2003, after observing the summer of negotiations between the Progressive Conservative and Canadian Alliance parties. It struck me then that what had transpired that summer between two conservative parties that had railed at each other for a decade needed to be put into a larger context. The final chapter was completed after the 2006 federal election. I hope, for the sake of the party and the country, that the lessons learned by carefully examining the events of these years will help prevent another such lost decade.

The perspective of this book is one of profound respect for the importance of the conservative idea in the dialectic of contemporary political debate. This perspective is tied not to any notion that conservatism must always prevail, but more properly to the premise that without the inclusion of the conservative idea, any debate that matters will be hollow and its outcome unreflective of society's broader and deeper interests and passions. My effort here is at once personal, because I have been an active partisan of the Conservative Party since my youth in the 1960s, and analytical, because my work outside of politics, in the private and not-for-profit sectors, has allowed me to see the conservative process from something other than the boundless optimism of the engaged partisan. These two strands come together in my deeply held view that the Conservative Party—sometimes loving, sometimes dysfunctional—is a family, not a private club. It is also an instrument for democratic government: whether in office or in opposition, the party is a public instrument with duties and obligations to the greater public welfare of Canada and Canadians.

One of the key Tory biases is a concern for balance. The absence of balance in political, intellectual, public, and corporate life inevitably leads to failure. Whether in the politics of the right, the left, or the centre, or in the business of investing and generating profit, or in the marketplace of ideas and insight, the absence of balance—of a measured reflection on the competing pressures at hand—is usually the precursor of a loss of legitimacy. Narrowness on the right or the left, too much intensity on the centralist or decentralist side in federal-provincial relations—these ordain incipient dysfunction. As I see it, the years from 1993 to 2006 represent a time when this balance within the Tory movement was disturbed by a period of hubris, fragmentation, incompetence, conceit, and a smaller view of our mission, a period that rendered a profound disservice to Canada.

Conservatism has its weaknesses, and they can be disruptive: fear of change, unvarnished belief in tradition, occasional distrust of collective endeavour, and deep tendencies toward division. (Robert Stanfield told me when I was a young legislative assistant that with three conservatives in a room, you would have at least five points of view.) But there is no doubt in my mind that these potential weaknesses are clearly outweighed by the beneficial presence of the conservative movement's root beliefs in individual opportunity balanced by the common interests of nation and enterprise and by the overarching framework of democratic freedom and institutional stability. This is the right counterbalance to the liberalism that de-emphasizes collective responsibility, thereby contributing to an atomized society in which individuals primarily seek their own material advance with little sense of responsibility, and in which anticipating the next trend outweighs understanding our history and protecting institutions that preserve order. Conservatism, therefore, has nothing less than a profound duty to the future: it is the duty of conservatives to understand and overcome the factionalist impulse in order not to default on this responsibility.

Allow me to set the political and geopolitical context of this study of one movement's recent travels and travails. Political causes and the parties and people that champion them have seasons, and there are histories on which these seasons are built. Those histories not only reach into the past, they also extend with unlimited impact into the future, shaping outcomes and strategies and being shaped in turn by personalities. The current dynamics of federal politics in Canada are not simply the result of the strengths and weaknesses of the present Conservative Party or the recent Jean Chrétien and Paul Martin ministries; they are also the result of a complex evolution over a number of years within a convergence of particular histories and contexts—an evolution not without connections to the wider post–Cold War conservative movement in the English-speaking world.

Conservative parties in the United Kingdom, the United States, and Canada have experienced more than just the ups and downs of political fortune since the fall of the Berlin Wall and the end of the Cold War. In all three countries, the politics of the conservative cause have been marked by internal dissent, dramatic change, and the dynamics of decision and reconciliation. Each of these twists and turns has created real consequences for individuals, policies, and society.

In the United Kingdom, the end of the Thatcher-Major era yielded a Conservative Party that was not so much in decline as in disarray, unable to present cohesive policies and coherent leadership at the same time. This disconnect from the British people not only enabled the rise of Tony Blair's New Labour centrism, but also afforded that movement room to grow on the right, as conservative political vacuums usually do. For Europe, for the transatlantic relationship, and for the geographical balance of the larger world, this conservative failure provided New Labour with great licence, one it has used with some long-term implications—some good, some less cheery—for British economic, military, and diplomatic policy. It is a licence that has contributed to challenges and reckonings as far away as Iraq, Sierra Leone, Washington, and Tripoli.

In American conservative politics, the period between Ronald Reagan and George W. Bush was one in which the promise of a post–Cold War new world order became, instead, the hard-slogging reality of commitments compromised, capacities overstretched, and naiveties shattered. The emergence of the Christian right in the core dynamics of the Republican Party, along with the isolationist Buchanan wing, conspired to dilute the patrician noblesse oblige of the Republican mainstream and shape a disparate coalition held together, from time to time, by overwhelming prospects for power and inexhaustible amounts of money. The despair during the Clinton years for American Republicans, along with the intensity of the character-assassinating excesses that changed the tone and intensity of American politics, also made a new candidate from Texas, with an old pedigree, the logical Republican option. The vicious attack on America and on innocent Americans by al-Qaeda produced a dynamic all its own within both Republican and Democratic circles. The Republican mindset into which that dynamic intruded so violently, however, was established as much by the conservative stresses within the Republican Party as by the broader political themes and arguments the party had come to embrace.

In Canada, the end of the Mulroney era ushered in a decade of fragmentation based on narrow ideology and regional discontent. Always a fragile and sometimes disenfranchised participant in Canadian politics, the conservative movement deserted the workable if temporary coalitions of leaders such as Diefenbaker, Stanfield, and Mulroney for the less worthy attractions of regional chauvinism, ideological excess, and disunity. At the beginning, in the late 1980s and early 1990s, Preston Manning led the forces of fragmentation, from the right of the conservative spectrum; in the new millennium, Joe Clark did so, from the left. As in the case of Great Britain with New Labour, these conceits and diversions gave licence to a Liberal Party in Canada to proceed unchallenged. Canada's facility, effectiveness, and competence diminished over a decade in areas as disparate as health care, defence, provincial fiscal capacity, and Canada-U.S. relations. The truth is, conservative self-indulgence was as much to blame for this state of affairs as were narrow or misguided Liberal policies. The anti-Quebec leanings during Mr. Manning's beginnings and the holier-than-thou Red Tory condescension of Joe Clark all helped and stoked the Liberal victory machine.

What is the impact on the quality of democracy when dysfunction and division dominate the conservative side of the debate? What price does a democracy pay in terms of ideas and the legitimacy of the democratic system itself? What are the genuine prospects for rebirth? What are the real implications for Canada and Canadians?

Part of the dynamism and promise of democratic capitalist societies comes from the very competencies and abilities of competing participants in the domestic politics and economics of those societies. The shape of free economies, equality of opportunity, tax policy, foreign and defence priorities, health care, and education, not to mention the core requirements of both economic productivity and social justice, are all determined in the end by spirited debate, by controversy, and by electoral battles that together produce both electoral outcomes at election time and political balance between elections. What happens when the conservative side defaults in its task, pushing federal voters to the "default" (Liberal) position? What price do we end up paying in the future? What are the negative forces that conservatism must confront if its contribution to the public good is to exceed its obsession with its internal demons? How do we get beyond the Liberal default position, and our own?

The broader public good requires setting aside the indulgence of ideological and regional nativism; conservatism is a force for good only when it has the courage to lead, balances nation and enterprise, and brings citizens together in deeply rooted common causes that respect the freedom to choose, a freedom inherent in all democratic societies.

When we choose ideological self-indulgence in our leadership or policy preferences, we forfeit the support of the vast majority of Canadians—or Americans, or Europeans—who are profoundly non-ideological. They seek governments that appear to understand the reality of people's lives, that have principled and realistic proposals to improve that reality, and that do so from philosophic principles that are both coherent and fair. Any party for whom its own ideological purity is more important than addressing reality on the ground not only forfeits but *deserves* to forfeit the chance to govern.

The conservative movement in Canada was to learn this the hard way, as this book lays out in somewhat gory detail.

PART 1

LOSING DIRECTION

1

A Fateful Choice

When it was announced that Prime Minister John George Diefenbaker would be coming to our parochial school and presenting a copy of the Canadian Bill of Rights to our principal, Dr. Melech Magid, and the United Talmud Torah Academy board president (and my great-uncle), Ben Beutel, I was quite excited. As I have also recalled in my book *No Surrender*, it was the early spring of 1962, and I was twelve years old, a grade-seven student at UTT, on St. Kevin Avenue in Montreal. To the north of this school and our secondary school, Herzliah High School, was the Spanish and Portuguese synagogue where I assisted Lionel Kaufman every Saturday at the junior congregation's Sabbath services. Kaufman was a distinguished gentleman with a British accent and an arm and leg in a brace, with which he walked laboriously. He always seemed to tear up as he read the Prayer for Queen and Country every Saturday after that week's Torah reading. Rabbi Solomon Frank, who was "in charge," told me on several occasions that "Lionel was a British fighter pilot who after many successful sorties, with Canadians, was shot down and seriously wounded over England—and had emigrated to Canada." Kaufman's belief that life was about duty, service, loyalty, faith, and freedom had an osmotic effect on me as a young congregational assistant. Rabbi Frank, meanwhile, meant much to both me and my family. After all, he was the Canadian Army chaplain who found my Uncle Max in a Canadian field hospital in Europe after he had been seriously wounded after charging the German lines with the Princess Louise Dragoon Guards at Monte Cassino in 1944.

I had never seen a prime minister before other than on television. Our riding was one that always voted Liberal (a classic rotten borough, Mount Royal), so it was clear that this visit was not aimed at pulling in a swing seat. I had no idea what to expect.

Our vice principal, Sadye Lewis (she of the heart-stopping whistle around the neck), had lectured us on the comportment a prime minister deserved from UTT students. "Anyone who misbehaves, does not come to school with pressed pants, or shows any lack of decorum will wear the embarrassment that he or she brings to UTT as a badge of shame forever." This was not just guilt—this was a preloaded, explosive guilt artillery shell aimed at one's entire structure of self-respect. So when the prime minister, the local Conservative candidate (Stan "The Man" Shenkman), the members of the UTT board, and Principal Magid entered the hall with other local worthies, while choirmaster Botvinik played a Haganah march on the upright piano, there was a definite air of expectancy.

I remember the PM's visit as if it were yesterday.

The welcoming speeches, the description of our school and its mission embellished for the prime minister's appreciation, the school choir's singing of "Land of the Silver Birch" after a rousing rendition of "God Save the Queen" and "Hatikvah"—all these passed without great moment. I noticed how Diefenbaker seemed to grow in stature as he sat through the part of Ben Beutel's introduction that stressed the 1961 passage by the Parliament of Canada—and the Diefenbaker government—of the Canadian Bill of Rights.

When Diefenbaker came to the podium in his dark blue pinstriped suit with a red, white, and blue tie and a handkerchief in his breast pocket, he referred to the folks on the stage respectfully. He mentioned Lionel Kaufman and his distinguished war service, and then he took his glasses off, set aside his text, looked out at all of us kids, and began:

> You young people are here, and are part of the Canadian family, because some of your parents and grandparents either chose Canada to build a life free of persecution and deprivation, and others among your parents fought in World War II to keep Canada free. They knew why they chose Canada, and were prepared to die for Canada. And they did that all so you could have a free Canada and make this country great.
>
> I know something of this school and what it is trying to do. I know that in your classrooms at the front of each class there is a large photograph of Her Majesty the Queen. I know that the idea here is that you spend half a day learning what all students learn—math, history, French, English literature, geography, composition—and in the other half you learn the Hebrew language, the Bible, the history of the Jewish people, the great

literature and stories of your people. I think that makes you better Canadians, and I think that makes Canada stronger.

You know, I could have used my mother's name from the British Isles of Bannerman. But I am a Diefenbaker—a Dutch name. I was born in an area of Dutch-German settlement in Ontario and have lived all my adult life in Saskatchewan. Out there we have many Canadians—French, Métis, Ukrainian, Polish, German, Dutch—and they are all Canadian to me. There were no French- or English- or Ukrainian- or Indian-Canadians on Juno Beach in 1944. They all wore the Canadian patch on their shoulder—they were all-Canadian, and all Canadians.

My government's Bill of Rights establishes once and for all, and for the first time as an Act of Parliament, that this is not a country where official discrimination for reasons of race, colour, creed, language, or land of origin will ever be tolerated.

This is a land where, whether your name is Kaufman or Diefenbaker, Baker or Mazankowski, Sevigny or Yuzyk, we are all welcome at the Canadian table. The Queen, our history, our democracy, our rights, our freedoms, are the property of every Canadian—however many syllables he has in his or her name. Whether working in a shirt factory in downtown Montreal, rising before the sun to milk the cows in eastern Ontario, working the combine till late at night on a prairie farm, or teaching school right here at UTT, this is your birthright, your heritage, your inheritance.

The idea of Canada, the ideas of our history and tradition, the idea that humble people can make great contributions, these make up the real idea of this country. This is what Canada is. Order, stability, freedom, a land of hope and opportunity, a place where government knows its place, a place where the freedom and spirit outside of government—on the family farm, the small business, the fishing boat, the corner store, the high school auditorium—is the spirit that inspires this great land. This is your country. Your parents have chosen it, strengthened it, defended it, and now, in you, they will continue it. They did not let you down. Canada did not let them down. Rich or poor, rural or urban, west or east, Christian or Jewish, this is who we are—and this is their inheritance.

Our duty—your duty? To keep it strong; to keep it free; to keep it a place of hope and opportunity. At the end of the Bill of Rights which I will now present to your principal, there is a final sentence that reads:

I am a Canadian, a free Canadian, free to speak without fear, free to worship God in my own way, free to stand for what I think right, free to oppose what I believe wrong, free to choose those who shall govern my country. This heritage of freedom I pledge to uphold for myself and all mankind.

Thank you all—and God bless you all!

We students were thunderstruck. The old men on the stage and the teachers had tears in their eyes—although few if any had ever voted Conservative. The waves of applause cascaded off the gym walls and the screen-mesh windows.

Miss Lewis stood at the microphone, and the whistle from the heights of Olympia blew. "Students, please rise for 'O Canada.'" Botvinik hit the introductory chords on the old upright and that anthem was sung with more force and emotion than I had ever heard before. (I did hear a more forceful version a few years later at the Montreal Forum, after the Junior Canadiens, with Jacques Plante in the net, beat the Moscow Selects with a comeback two goals in the last three minutes of the game.)

Emotionally, for me, that sealed the deal. If that was what conservatism meant—tradition, respect for diversity, a strong sense of Canada as a family, a pan-Canadian view of what we meant to each other, a duty to the past, a respect for faith and history, a frankness about discrimination and a will to fight it, a sense that the state had a role to play but ought to know its place, the understanding that it was not in government that societies were built but out in schoolyards, homes, churches, factories, farms, coastal fisheries, and small businesses—then I was a conservative, and a Conservative.

My enthusiasm that night at Friday dinner was met with a stern rebuke from my dad. After all, he was a lifelong Liberal and a poll captain for Milton Klein, the Liberal MP for the riding of Cartier. It was met with loving derision by my grandfather, a tailor in a women's cloak factory, an NDP supporter, and a long-time supporter of the International Ladies' Garment Workers' Union, having been a shop steward for many years. My mom, meanwhile, was conciliatory, eager not to have a political row ruin the Friday night meal. She urged me to write all four parties (including the Social Credit Party of Canada, then led by Robert Thompson) for information before making a final choice.

I learned several things from that event and its aftermath. Conservatism, I could see, was a minority taste, certainly in the Montreal where I grew up, though being in the minority did not mean being in the wrong. Conservatism, I began to sense, was concerned with history, hope, and inclusion. I saw that when it reached out, it could inspire and motivate, and when it did not, it would be outsold by hope nine times out of ten.

I learned in the Montreal of the 1960s that the Canadian establishment was deeply Liberal, and that while this was not without good reason, the establishment was not always right. I learned that Liberalism was the establishment view because Conservatives were outsiders, or because the establishment felt safer with the Liberal Party and its approach to the role, nature, and purpose of government.

Over time, as I read Disraeli and Churchill and pondered the writings of Michael Oakeshott and Donald Creighton and even the work of William F. Buckley, Jr., I realized that the "tyranny of the idea" and its importance to conservatives made us idealists of the most naive kind: idealists regarding the right mix of history, order, and freedom, and idealists regarding the tough choices that voters could be asked to make. Our realism about society, about affordability, about the communist enemy during the Cold War, about the value of tradition, parliamentary democracy, and Canadian sovereignty (when we opposed the Americans on the Bomarc missile issue and after the Bay of Pigs) made us easy pickings for Lester Pearson and the U.S.-assisted Liberal Party campaign of 1963.

Over time, I realized that Diefenbaker—who was outstanding in front of high school audiences and who answered the letters of twelve- and thirteen-year-olds (I had dutifully written following my mother's counsel) with sincere, personally signed letters—was less than perfect in how he led his government and party, creating many of his own problems. His focus on control and his disdain for the press launched forces that were eventually trained on him, causing his downfall. Yet he came, he fought, he won, he stood, and he was formidably defeated. The populism of his appeal, the honesty of his approach to public life, and his identification with the average person on the street were the traits of a man who had gone up against the establishment of his own party and Bay Street and who, in 1958, had won the greatest majority to that point in our history.

The chord he struck in me transcended party affiliation to create a vision of our nation's soul, our country's real personality, unbuffed and unmanaged. How that soul is nurtured in different political traditions and cultures is part of the classic modern challenge facing a range of conservative leaders.

That populist tinge was certainly not where I began my conservative journey. My early connection to the populism and inclusion of the Diefenbaker brand of Prairie conservatism was, however, a very real constraint on my deeply held biases of a more Tory sort. Coming from the most humble of working-class origins, my biases had and have little to do with aristocracy, at least not in any personal sense. They come more from my sense of order and continuity and how vital they both are to genuine freedom and community.

The front of every class in my grade school was festooned with drawings (obviously not from memory) of various Old Testament prophets and personages: Joseph, Moses, Aaron, King David, King Solomon, Jeremiah, Ezekiel, and the rest of the great and sometimes holy. At the centre, and above, was always a photograph of Queen Elizabeth II and Prince Philip (he in his Royal Navy uniform). When I inquired in grade four why this photo was in the place of honour, the response of my home room teacher, Mrs. Handelman, was, "Because under the Crown, we are all equal before the law, which is why we are free to practise our faith and worship freely in Canada."

This was before Diefenbaker's 1961 Bill of Rights. In a school whose ranks included both immigrant and first-generation Canadian teachers and students, and the children of Holocaust survivors, this was a significant consensus. The lone dissenter was an Israeli import who taught Hebrew grammar and literature and who brought the late-1940s anti-British bias of many of his Israeli generation to our classroom. I viewed his ramblings as just that—and as profoundly un-Canadian and ahistorical. I believed then, and continue to believe, that the notion that any other colonial power would have withdrawn with as much civility or grace as the British did is pure fantasy. (Imagine the Russian, German, French, or Chinese in a similar circumstance. They would have been the imperials who never left.)

I am reminded of being in a large crowd and sitting on Dad's shoulders (I was five and a half) on the day in 1956 that Queen Elizabeth arrived in a huge Cadillac to visit our city hall, Hôtel de Ville d'Outremont, a Georgian building of some character on Côte Ste-Catherine. Her Majesty was in Montreal as part of the celebration of the opening of the St. Lawrence Seaway, which she and President Eisenhower would rightly commemorate as one of the great engineering wonders of the world. The Queen used the time to visit Quebec and Ontario, no doubt encouraged by a St. Laurent government that was both royalist and facing an election in a year or so.

Now, one does not feel fully integrated into the larger society when one grows up in an immigrant family where Yiddish is spoken at the dinner table by one's parents and relatives, where the children attend parochial school, where attendance at an Orthodox synagogue is normal and regular, where one's house is strictly kosher, and where one's entire circle of friends and relatives are of the same faith and from the same part of

Eastern Europe. In fact, I suspect that for every generation of immigrants, the demi-world of "our own kind" is the formative experience from which some never emerge. The demi-world can be at once a place of support and welcome and, over time, a prison from which escape is either impossible or emotionally very expensive.

J. J. Zlotnick was the rabbi-in-chief of the near Beth Moishe synagogue at Durocher and Lajoie in lower Outremont, where we grew up. He was not without humour, but he could rain down fire and brimstone over the risks of intermarriage—and of losing the purity of one's faith and failing to observe the six hundred plus daily commandments that an observant Orthodox Jew was to try to perform. (Because no one, in the modern age, could come close to performing more than about half of them, the daily guilt of incompetence and failure dogged our every step. This is something some Catholics and Presbyterians would instantly recognize in their own religious experience.) Whatever his many gifts as pastoral guide and orator, a passionate proponent of integration he was not—in fact, if anything, he created a sense that simply chatting with a gentile was a step down the slippery slope.

Yet I remember looking at the platform of local worthies awaiting Her Majesty's arrival—the mayor, the local MP and town councillors, and the MNA were there. The local clergy, both French and English, were out in force: Catholic, Anglican, and Greek Orthodox priests; local Protestant clergy; and, in the last row, with homburg hat and bespectacled round face and funeral suit, our rabbi. There he was, actually sitting next to and perhaps even rubbing the odd shoulder with clergy of other faiths. And, as my dad explained to me, the person about to arrive was not only the head of the Commonwealth—the person we rejoiced over while singing "God Save the Queen"—but also the titular head of the Church of England.

The Queen was welcomed by the federal minister and the local militia colonel and took the salute, then she proceeded to the platform and addressed the large crowd in flawless French and English—but not until she had shaken every hand on the platform and had a brief word with each person there assembled. Her Majesty shook Rabbi Zlotnick's hand, and they spoke for what seemed like an hour but was probably thirty seconds or fewer. I was mesmerized. By an act of simple royal courtesy, Elizabeth II had redefined community for me, and what being a Canadian (as opposed to being a Russian immigrant's son living in Canada) actually meant. In subsequent Sabbath services I would pester the rabbi for what the Queen had said. His response, spoken with some nobility and aloofness, was always, "Hugh, it is not appropriate to disclose the sovereign's comments." I noticed that the Prayer for Queen and Country was moved up during the service from next-to-last to right after the Torah scroll was returned to the ark: a very honoured place in the liturgy.

It was after the prime minister's speech at my school in 1962 that I made my fateful choice to be conservative and Conservative. I say "fateful" because my choice has taken me on a fascinating pilgrimage at once frustrating and fulfilling, from youthful idealism and partisanship to the experiences recorded in this book that were part of the Conservative Party's long road back to power. Forged in me through my early experiences was my deep and abiding sense that it was from history and institutional stability—from the generations that linked through the ages to the origins of our laws and constitution—that freedom comes. The Queen could well have simply made a speech, performed the usual walkabout, and moved on. Instead, a hand from an individual—and a link directly to Magna Carta— was extended, and communities were touched and united to be part of the larger historical reality of this then young Dominion.

Part of the conservative mission in modern society is to shape the future out of a sense of common duty to the past—to the people: some royal, some made up of those who sacrificed themselves in peace and war, some who built and broadened, some who worked honourably and paid their taxes and defined street-level civility. This may be elitist in that we celebrate those who volunteered to serve as opposed to those who abdicated their duty, and we celebrate those who toiled and achieved as opposed to those for whom the selfish pursuits were all there was. But it is also profoundly conservative. It is a mission that can be tolerant of what is new and fashionable in our politics, while also being deeply discerning. There are core institutions and values that, while not perfect, must be sustained, largely because there is no alternative with which to replace them.

These are the mileposts of our way ahead. If we do not follow them, the possibility of mayhem and disintegration truly increases—a reality in which excessive self-regard replaces concerns about the public good. One thing is true of American politics, both of the anti-war left (they usually oppose all wars—until they see how they go) and of the anti-government far right, who have institutionalized selfishness (to paraphrase Sir Keith Joseph's comment about socialism): that disengagement from the past is nearly total among their respective prophets.

The essential Tory is not, and never has been, defined by right or left; he or she is concerned with tradition, lineage, civility, and balance—something Margaret Thatcher did not fully understand. Something the neocon mind cannot really grasp. Something the Canadian Liberal—that curious creature to whom we turn next in attempting to understand the reality that Conservatives always face—is too consumed with trends to actually even notice.

2

The Default Reality

Of course, I did not realize at the time that the road I had picked for myself—or that had picked me—would lead me into periods of wilderness experience. I was to learn pretty quickly, however, that federally, I had picked the nomadic side. I say this because the default position for Canadian voters has not really changed since the defeat of Sir John A. Macdonald in 1871 over the Pacific Scandal. It is the position of choosing, more often than not, the supposedly managerially competent Liberals over any other option. It is the position of choosing the Liberals and their confidence and coherence about maintaining power over the often idea-driven Conservatives, who, on the core concerns of competent government, internal unity, and focus, seem less resolute than Liberals.

Conservatives such as Robert Stanfield, Joe Clark, Kim Campbell, Jean Charest, Preston Manning, and Stockwell Day have all been sent packing at one level or another by Canadian voters. This was not always because their ideas were extreme. Often it was because they could not portray even the most rudimentary patina of competence and coherence. In 1993, the Liberals' Jean Chrétien offered hope. We, in contrast, offered a mismanaged campaign and an awkward callousness about hope. In 1997, we offered compelling national leadership in Charest but a stunningly irresolute lack of clarity on the rules going forward regarding any Quebec referendum. In 2000, we received, under Clark, the lowest percentage of PC votes ever recorded, with the Reform-Alliance part of the conservative family doing its best ever under Day.

The current Stephen Harper government notwithstanding, we have achieved a remarkable run of institutional and electoral irrelevance. And what is even worse than irrelevance? A lack of party unity and a tendency toward extremism—toward radical, overly simple solutions to complex policy problems. For example, Clark's well-meaning embrace, in 1979, of a new Canadian embassy in Jerusalem, the result of hollow pandering as opposed to solid diplomatic initiative, spoke deeply of an apparent lack of simple political skill. The lack of internal discipline in the 2004 election produced outbreaks of anti–Charter of Rights, anti-choice, and homophobic excess, helping the Liberals retain power one election more than was necessary.

These two factors not only render a political party essentially unelectable, but further aggravate and corrode the basis of a competitive democracy. When a political party gets to this point, it has stopped harming itself and begun harming the country and its people. This is, unfortunately, where we were before the 2005 party conference in Montreal.

I make no secret of the fact that I have voted Conservative all my life. I have served as the chair of the 2004 transition-planning committee, as well as in a host of senior roles, and I even sought the leadership of the party in 1998, against Clark. From this perspective, it was important for me to try to understand what it is that keeps Canadians running back to a federal Liberal government.

When Conservatives come around who break the mould, such as John Diefenbaker or Brian Mulroney, the level of establishment angst and vilification implies that Conservative government is simply an unnatural state of affairs, one that the very rhythms of Mother Earth require to be corrected as soon as possible. The fact that Conservative governments often contribute to a rapid return to the Liberals is one manifestation of how the default position renders Conservatives profoundly inexperienced in government, which itself becomes a circular and self-fulfilling prophecy.

After a long decade of such frustration, the question needs to be asked: Does Canada need the Conservatives? Is Canada essentially a one-party state with anyone other than the Liberals present merely to legitimize a democratic process whose result is essentially predictable 90 per cent of the time? Is it really the role of the NDP simply to pull the Liberals to the left on occasion in order to keep Liberals campaigning from the left while governing from the right? Is it really the role of Conservatives—whether fragmented or united—to exemplify what Liberals and most moderate Canadians oppose so that election after election becomes a sort of *Groundhog Day* recasting of Liberal restoration?

Is there something endemic to the premises, history, or essence of the Conservatives that makes the Conservative option unacceptable to Canadians? Is there something fundamentally more decent, fair, honest, or reasonable about the Liberals that makes them far more acceptable and comfortable? Or do the Conservatives suffer from a deficit in the core competencies of government, political organization, policy development, or leadership that has caused success to elude them?

This question is not simply about the strengths and weaknesses of the present Conservative Party or the dynamic of the recent Paul Martin ministry. It arises from the history, context, and evolution of the post-Mulroney decade—an evolution not without linkages to the wide post–Cold War conservative movement in the English-speaking world. To suggest in rural Leeds County, for example, that the representation of that seat in Parliament from 1988 to 2004 by a Liberal—despite the intensely conservative, Orange, and Protestant nature of so many in its community—had as much to do with conservative fragmentation in the later years or with the preservation of milk marketing boards in the earlier years may seem far-fetched, but the truth of the matter is that both factors counted, not only in Leeds, but throughout vote- and seat-rich Ontario, in ways it is important to understand.

A nation of voters who seem comfortable only with this default position are guilty of no serious sin; they are letting no one down but themselves. It's just that the Liberal default position seems to them very much the least harmful of the choices available. Surely this is a reasonable choice within a democratic "rational choice" framework. Nevertheless, Conservatives need to ask themselves how the core, substance, and demeanour of their offering help shape this popular default choice. They need to ask how much of that total Conservative offering is indulgent and unbalanced. How much of it is more concerned with internal fence-mending than with serving the public? How competent are the policy and governance choices being offered to Canadians? The question is whether Canadians, rather than simply retreating to a safe default position as they did through 2004, are actually seeing something intrinsically unbalanced or disconnected from reality in the Conservative Party of the new millennium.

Conservatives cannot, however, take all the blame for the Liberals' continued dominance. The Liberals, for their part, have shown a remarkable ability to cling to power. An important component of this success has been their marked willingness to modify their ideology as the times warrant. In contrast, while Conservatives and New Democrats may disagree intensely on how best to buttress individual freedom, collective responsibility, and equality of opportunity within society, they both stay firmly rooted in their ideologies. These two parties have had rank-and-file and elite members who have been more loyal to ideas and principles than to their fellow party members or leaders. Both Conservatives and New Democrats begin with views of society that, while different, are absolutely organic. Both view societies as composites of individuals, institutions, communities, and histories that are irrevocably linked to each other and dependent on each another. While Conservatives and New Democrats disagree intensely on how best to maximize individual freedom, collective responsibility, and equality of opportunity within society, they both see society as an integrated whole.

Democracies and the quality of choices they make in every area of public policy—from child care to defence, from agricultural subsidies to energy exports—are made more effective by open and heated competition by opposing political parties and opposing philosophies of government. It is an integral part of our history that the range of differences on the left-right spectrum has not been very wide. The difference between moderate Conservatives such as Bill Davis or Peter Lougheed and moderate New Democrats such as Bob Rae or Gary Doer have never been very broad. In the United Kingdom, differences between Ted Heath and Margaret

Thatcher were much, much larger in terms of the role and purpose of government itself. The Liberals' amazing political success, however, has been the result of their mastery of tactical flexibility. For them, to take a stand on a particular issue—right or left—is to reduce tactical political and policy options. They are deeply unburdened by conviction.

If a core philosophical coherence was at the centre of one's view of society as a whole, one could not oppose a wage and price freeze in the 1974 election only to impose it several months thereafter, as Trudeau did. One could not oppose the Canada-U.S. Free Trade Agreement, NAFTA, and the GST in one political cycle, only to embrace all three in the next cycle—under Prime Minister Chrétien.

Giving voters what they appear to want in return for continued re-election is, of course, a time-honoured tradition of which no political party is utterly innocent. But it is not without consequences.

I was part of the negotiations between the provinces and Ottawa on the patriation of the Constitution in 1981–82, as associate cabinet secretary in Ontario, federal-provincial relations. The issue of the Charter of Rights and Freedoms was central to Trudeau's strategy. The Charter was deeply rooted in the Trudeauesque—individual affirmation, flower children, opposition to the Vietnam War, pirouettes behind the Queen's back, and all the other adolescent hallmarks of Trudeau's hold on Canadians. It had also been exhaustively polled across various key voter groups in the Liberal voter coalition. Furthermore, senior advisers to Trudeau, such as Michael Kirby and James Coutts, understood viscerally that few premiers would want to campaign openly against a charter of rights in their own province.

While I did trust the frankness and openness of these two gentlemen, Kirby and Coutts, I had very little regard for the motivation or integrity of their leader. In my view, Trudeau was guilty of the worst, bar none, human and civil rights abuse since World War II. Under the War Measures Act, invoked in October 1970, he detained, arrested, and imprisoned hundreds of Quebeckers—many arrested in the middle of the night—not one of whom was ever charged with any crime.

I was a student government leader at the University of Ottawa at the time, in the fall semester of 1970, and I saw friends and acquaintances arrested and detained for days and weeks simply because their names were on a Parti Québécois list. I saw police officers go from room to room in our student government building on Laurier Boulevard, searching for filing cabinets with lists of members. Trudeau deserted everything he had stood for when he had written for *Cité Libre* and took on Duplessis. In fact, Duplessis in comparison was a mildly eccentric nationalist whose human rights violations would hardly register on the Richter scale.

In the negotiations, Trudeau was petulant and often insulting, even to allies Richard Hatfield and Bill Davis. He was prepared to end the talks prematurely and force a referendum, to use the Charter as leverage against all the premiers—a charter based on the principle of freedom of association that had, since World War II, been violated only by Trudeau himself. Liberals embraced the Charter because it would mobilize their overall constitutional package. Davis and Hatfield supported it because it would help francophone minorities in their provinces and the anglophone minority in Quebec and—they thought—serve to constrain government from its worse excesses.

But like the unnecessary use of the War Measures Act in 1970 (there were other less draconian options, such as local martial law or curfews, as my old friend, then Conservative Party president, Nathan Nurgitz wrote in *Strong and Free*, a response to the War Measures Act), the use of the Charter as leverage in 1982 would presage a rebirth of support for

Quebec sovereignty and assist the sovereigntists in isolating Quebec from the constitutional mainstream. At one level, Premier René Lévesque could not have signed any agreement that affirmed the federalist super-structure that included Quebec. At another, the Liberals were so wed to politics-by-poll that they could not actually find another way to reach out to Quebec without harming Trudeau's appeal in English Canada—most notably established by his resolute if dismissive attendance at the Saint-Jean-Baptiste nationalist parade on the eve of the 1968 election—as being the Quebec politician who could stand up to the province.

To be sure, conservatives (and Conservatives) bring a principled framework—a core structural and organic view of society—to their world view: the role of tradition, history, stability, order, and the rule of law as necessary precursors of freedom and opportunity; the role of enterprise and profit in the generation of social mobility and justice; the role of the nation state as a global interlocutor concerning the values and principles Canadians hold dear; the role of the family and faith as positive forces even in the most pluralist and secular societies. These principles shape our approach to policy, our belief in government and local industry. It is a structural framework that sets us apart from Liberal flexibility—which often knows no bounds at all.

To some extent, the latter's resounding defeat across the country in 1984—just two years after these constitutional negotiations—was a result of both their de facto isolation of Quebec in 1982 and their imposition of per-gallon tax increases on gasoline in the post-1980 period far higher than the eighteen-cents-per-gallon decision Clark was defeated for in the House of Commons at the end of 1979.

When Richard Hatfield was premier of New Brunswick during a period of leadership on social policy, the Charter of Rights, and the patriation of the Constitution, we all knew that he owned three wardrobes. One was for the size he was at election time, one was for between elections, and one was for the pre-election diet period. Liberals have simply taken this principle and applied it more broadly across policy choices, with the size and colour of the policy-fashion shaped by the *sondage du jour*. One can be condescending about this lack of principle and values in our national decision-making. Many of us have indulged in pointing this out, on issues from the missile-defence decision by Martin to the Iraq decision by Chrétien. But in a democracy, being in sync with the public mood—a stance requiring little character and even less genuine leadership and advocacy—is not, in and of itself, necessarily a sin. Les Horswill, a senior policy adviser in Ontario's Ministry of Treasury, Economics, and Intergovernmental Affairs in the 1980s, used to say that there was "nothing so elegant as giving inspired advice that is not taken." He may well have been right, but in the day-to-day competition between democratic political parties, having one's options for Canada's future consistently rejected leads to irrelevance, and worse.

It is also vital to understand the world view of Canada's federal Liberals and the damage that results when we give the Liberals too much power. The Liberals focus on federal government. They have little if any role in provincial government in entire regions of the country and at best an alternating role in the central and eastern regions. Part of the Ottawa Disease, therefore, is a view of Canada as a strict federation, in which Ottawa, fiscally and otherwise, sails on its own sea. One result is that the federal government is literally awash in financial liquidity, while just about every Canadian province outside Alberta is either fighting a large deficit or propping up an uneasy budgetary balance. More generally, the disease is a profound denial of the confederal reality of a country whose constitution cries out for more partnership in areas of mutual jurisdiction among the federal and provincial and municipal levels.

In the self-reverential Liberal view, the level at which they are governing is automatically the centre of the universe. Issues that may matter to people in their day-to-day lives are seen by federal Liberals from a central-government viewpoint. The notion that other levels of government or, heaven forbid, bodies outside of government may have a critical role to play in choosing their own priorities simply does not come up.

It is a view of Canada and Confederation that is profoundly unproductive and harmful. We are not a unitary state. I remember adjudicating a national essay contest in 1994 in which undergraduate university students were to write on the priorities for Canada they would pursue were they to become prime minister. My fellow judges in that year—Rob Prichard, the president of the University of Toronto; Jack Webster of the Vancouver media world; and Belinda Stronach, then of Magna (whose Fair Enterprise Institute was sponsoring the nationwide endeavour)— were impressed with the overall quality and careful thinking in what they read. The only disturbing trend, largely among students in the sciences and often among those who happened not to have been born here, was references to the need to simplify government and to do away with the provinces. I patiently explained, as we crossed the country, that, well, the provinces had *created* Canada and not the other way around. I mentioned that the essential balance between sections 91 and 92 of the British North America Act was vital to the founding of Confederation and modern Canada. Liberals often show the same callous misunderstanding of the confederal balance that is necessary to sustain the Canadian idea.

The Chrétien era was typified by a father-knows-best style of federalism, one that was not challenged, as it could have been, by a dynamic, more confederal approach to national problem solving. There was no meaningful consultation with the provinces when the Liberals introduced the Canada Health and Social Transfer as a way of slashing transfer payments to the provinces, imposing a cap—which, to be fair, Tories had begun to put in place—on the Canada Assistance Program and thereby hobbling the capacity of provinces such as Ontario to sustain welfare rolls deepened by the Liberal-inspired recession. It was deeply inflationary year-over-year spending increases by Premier David Peterson in Ontario that forced Governor Crowe to ramp up interest rates to slow inflationary pressures in the 1985–1990 period. This fed the recessionary pressures that plagued Bob Rae in the post-1990 period, under Conservative and Liberal federal governments. Here was a real chance for cooperation between Finance Minister Martin and the provinces—but it never really came. That there was a national fiscal problem Ottawa and that the provinces, as partners in Confederation, might join forces to address it seems not to have occurred to the Chrétien administration, or to Paul Martin as finance minister. The burden was simply passed to the provinces.

We should give Martin the immense credit he deserves as finance minister between 1993 and 2002 (along with Prime Minister Chrétien, who, despite their differences, supported his minister of finance's policies in a remarkably steadfast way) for having stemmed the fiscal run that was threatening our economic and international standing. It is important to note, however, that Martin did so largely at the expense of national defence and the provinces. Some in Ottawa will argue that this one-third reduction in provincial transfers was not that extensive if you count the tax points transferred to the provinces over the years. It seems fair to conclude, however, that serious capacity issues were created in health care and social programs across the country because of Ottawa's cuts, and that those serious declines were based on diminished provincial capacity, tax points included.

The mere fact that the billions of dollars cut by the federal government in transfers to the provinces in the mid-1990s were essentially put back in at the beginning of the next decade through a series of health accords and some boutique federal investments—the Canadian Foundation for Innovation, the Canada Research Chairs at the universities, the Medical Research Council, Canada Health Infoway, the Canadian Institute for Health Information, the Millennium Scholarships, to name but a few— reveals a fair amount about Liberal strategy and approach.

One cannot but praise the many federal initiatives in medical research and university support, or the relative generosity in the health accords that reinvested so much. The new federal initiatives, such as the ones mentioned above, while all of considerable merit, had no provincial financial consultation in their design or structure. It is clear that this was Ottawa acting on its own—first to cut, then to reinvest. The provinces were at the table twice with Chrétien in the decade of 1993–2003, mostly near the end of that period, and some consultation did take place. In the end, however, the health-accord dynamic was one of Ottawa putting back money it had already cut and the provinces accepting the money because they had no other choice. It was not an exercise in collaborative federalism.

There was even less consultation between the two levels of government in the run-up to the 1995 Quebec Referendum. The total collapse of whatever the federal strategy may have been was in some measure built on an admonition from Chrétien's office to the premiers to stay out. Not even Trudeau in 1980 had that kind of arrogance.

It's useful to contrast this Chrétien Liberal approach to the 1995 crisis with another example. In 1980, at the time of the first Quebec referendum, premiers such as Davis, Lougheed, and Hatfield went to Quebec, undertaking that they would work with Quebeckers toward constitutional change within Confederation if Quebeckers voted "no" to sovereignty. This was done with the approval of Claude Ryan, the PLQ leader and leader of the *non* forces in Quebec, and with the knowledge and support of the PMO. As a member of Bill Davis's team in 1980, I liaised directly with Pierre Pettigrew, who was then Ryan's chief of staff. This was Canada at its best, involved in a difficult democratic engagement but one in which there was common cause.

In 1995, however, Chrétien's federalism had no space for common cause, or even common communication. As the pro-Canada numbers began to collapse in Quebec in 1995 and premiers across the country became more concerned, it was almost impossible to get hard information out of Ottawa. As a dollar-a-year constitutional adviser to Premier Harris in Ontario, I saw at first hand the Ontario frustration over the lack of any inclusive Ottawa approach to the possible crisis. It was as if Ottawa had become a spectator at the potential dissolution of Canada itself and was consigning the provinces to the orange seats up in the most remote corner of the arena. The only problem was, the game on the ice was about *Canada,* and everybody, not just the federal Liberal government, had a stake in the outcome.

When Premier Harris took his son to the final large demonstration for Canada in Montreal with other premiers and Canadians from all walks of life, and when Charest spoke for Canadians, it was essentially a raid on the gold seats by the Canadians in the grey and orange seats, who wanted to show love of country, respect for Quebec's key and critical differences and requirements, and their own desire to help. On referendum night, as Ontario considered what financial market and international debt market confidence issues it might have to address the next morning, Ottawa's presence was still somewhat disengaged.

Space does not allow me to detail the many other examples of Liberal myopia and arrogance, including the chronic underfunding of defence and amateurish handling of Canada-U.S. relations. However, it is fascinating, in this regard, to see how Prime Minister Chrétien engaged the provinces after the crisis of September 11, 2001—or did not. The horror of the terrorist attacks on New York City and Washington caught all governments by surprise, and the Canadian government's rapid response in the safe landing of so many aircraft and passengers diverted from American destinations was of immense value. Clearly, however, the prime minister's instinct was to sustain normalcy and the appearance of normalcy by holding no extraordinary emergency meetings. There was a sense of underengagement that, in view of the proximity and the "in the family" nature of the target (not to mention the Canadians killed at the World Trade Center towers), is difficult to understand. The slowing of the border on September 12 by the Americans was as clear a sign of a potential national emergency as one might economically anticipate. Was there a conference call from Ottawa with the premiers? Were there even meetings between emergency measures ministers? The first real sign of leadership in the public domain was a statement some days later by John Manley, then minister of foreign affairs and deputy prime minister, who indicated that there were cemeteries all over the world where Canadians lay, having fallen in defence of freedom and in loyalty to our allies, and that we would not be deserting our allies now.

Individual premiers made their own decisions to dispatch aid to New York; Premier Harris of Ontario, for example, sent coroner, medical, and first-responder support. Individual firefighters and units headed down to New York, but a coordinated federal-provincial engagement or even consultation? Not a whiff of it.

This approach spoke volumes to the insularity of the federal government when controlled by Liberals. Not even a potential national emergency justified reaching out to the provinces—in spite of the fact that the provinces have, with their cities and towns, the primary first-responder duty in cases of fire, health, national emergency, environment, and police emergency.

In the competitive world of party politics, competence matters. And competence in the fractiousness of Canadian politics includes keeping a disparate political party together, as Chrétien found out the hard way in the new millennium. Conservatives as a national force have mattered only when their reach was national, their spectrum broad, and the range of strongly held opposing views met squarely with both accommodation and leadership. Successful prime ministers and putative prime ministers in any conservative party manage this well, or they manage not at all. Offering Canadians something different and credible after a decade of Liberal political dominance would be possible only if a truly national accommodating conservative force could be forged.

This was a key reality that a growing group of conservatives in both the Alliance and the Progressive Conservative parties began to understand after the horrific election of 2000 that elected a third Liberal majority, and reduced the Tories under Clark to their lowest popular vote ever.

3

THE FORCES OF FRAGMENTATION

When campaigning for Parliament as a young candidate in downtown Ottawa for Stanfield in 1972, I was met at many doors by older public servants who deeply resented the Official Languages Act and were convinced that their own careers had tapered off as a result. They resented even more Stanfield's support of the act, and my loyal support of Stanfield's and the party's position on the issue.

In a country with a sparse population and large regional geographies, government, as a brokerage agent between legitimate regional interests, is an easy whipping boy. Atlantic Canada's strong sense of grievance, the wealthy west's sense of being put upon and unfairly excluded from the decision-making process, Quebec's traditional objections to federal incursions into its area of constitutional authority, Ontario's anxieties about the amount of federal tax collected and redistributed from its economy—all form the superstructure of complaint that defines our politics. Conservatives are easily engaged if not snared by this regional narrative, because we care more intensely than Liberals about the British North America Act's balance, in sections 91 and 92, of the core legislative infrastructure of Confederation, which means we care about local and provincial rights and prerogatives and tend—in peacetime, anyway—to be more decentralizing than Liberals or socialists.

However, our attention to the infrastructure of complaint does not mean we have abandoned our traditional Tory view of and respect for government. This view, in both its normative and its dysfunctional manifestations, is best understood in the context of Tory history and trends in the UK and the United States as well as in Canada.

The deep-seated anti-government bias that often attends upon conservative groups is not central to Canadian Toryism. It is more a part of American neoconservative excess. It has become part of the anti-Washington "all government is evil" battle cry often associated, fairly or unfairly, with such nativists as Pat Buchanan and the more extreme elements of the American conservative direct-mail anti-government coalition so dominant in aspects of the GOP. The popularization of American conservatism has brought with it both good and bad. The good had been a vigorous internal debate between conservatives everywhere about the purposes of their cause and the goals of their movement. The roots of American neoconservatism are, intellectually, northeastern American liberal and Democrat: think Patrick Moynihan, Norman Podhoretz, Irving Kristol, and others from that narrow circle. Their departure from mainstream liberalism was tied to the *crise du jour* challenges of both anti-Semitism in aspects of the black activist movement and the

growing anti-Israel sentiment among some traditional left-liberal opponents of the Vietnam War. It was also partly in response to the intense
liberal myopia concerning Soviet excesses in Eastern Europe, including
against the Russian people. It does not change the fact that those who
went from centre left to a more pronounced right were liberals to begin
with. They brought with them that unique brand of American liberalism
that stemmed from the excesses of the American Revolution itself and
from the clear preference of the Founding Fathers to structure a governance system for America and Americans that preferred the employment
of countervailing powers to the British model of unified governance.
Distrust of so-called efficient government was understandable when
the new America was emerging in 1776, with musket and blood, from
what the colonists saw as a tyranny imposed from afar. Their distrust of
the British became a systemic distrust of government overall. The real
purpose of the U.S. division of powers was the *dilution* of powers. The
premise behind the separation of powers, and even behind the separation
of church and state, was to contain the power of the state and leave unfet-
tered in society as a whole the role of religion and the broad spectrum of
private association it inspires.

This essentially American view of liberalism has been and remains a
dynamic force around the world, a force that exalts the individual, that
abhors the state, and that exalts the citizen as hunter-gatherer and warrior. It is a strong force for human rights, individual freedom, and, on
some days, religious tolerance, both at home and abroad. In moderation,
it can be a force for good. Without balance, however, it can become its
own tyranny.

Beyond being a tyranny, its proponents can and do discredit all government in ways that are profoundly disingenuous about the excesses of

the private sector. To hear David Frum rage on about the corruption of Liberals or to read his well-argued pieces in the *National Post* during the last election campaign in Canada, one could only conclude that to be in government, in Canada, and a Liberal was to be corrupt—none of which is, of course, necessarily true: corrupt politicians may be found in every government of every stripe. Frum's tone was driven not only by a sincere sense of outrage, but also by the chance to discredit government itself, and those who serve in it. Given the recent Conservative victory, this excess is bound to produce a blowback that may make it impossible for even the most honest of Conservative politicians to manage while in office.

We must remember that it is utterly outside both the Tory and the broader conservative traditions to devalue government. The majesty in Canada of the inherited British ethic with respect to government, which was merged with the focus on culture, language, and religion of the *ancien régime,* is that government was and is a civil instrument for both accommodation and progress—and both accommodation and progress are absolutely essential to the developing Canadian experience. Accommodation between the English and French, among the different regions, classes, and interests, and with our First Nations, is at the soul of the Canadian experience. It is why we did not have a civil war, why we have universal health care, why we have both federal and provincial jurisdiction. Dismissing all government as corrupt and all politicians as dishonest plays to the jealousies and petty biases of those who find it easy to blame government for their own failings.

But the peaceable kingdom sought by traditional conservatives of the British and Canadian tradition is not based on government. It is, rather, based on the twin weights of nation and enterprise, giving a sense of the broader community that productive societies must embrace if there are to be the values, trust, stability, and order from which true freedom and opportunity come. Government has a genuine role to play in this dynamism of enterprise, and benefits immensely from it. For the Tory, nation and enterprise are equally essential. In neoliberal/neoconservative practice, the market is the all-pervasive and central framework of life, because it is the ultimate counterweight to the forces of the state; the more traditional conservative view places the market alongside the key pillars of society: history, family, faith, freedom, the rule of law, nation (in the old days, empire), all linked in an organic union in which there are rules, boundaries, common values, and common cause. This organic relationship—this belief that society is not a series of atomized pieces, with no duties to the common ideal, to each other, or to the nation as a whole—is what allows conservatives and socialists to respect each other while disagreeing fundamentally on the key organizing economic principles of society. Disagreeing over what the principles should be is not the same as disagreeing over whether there should be any principles at all. Here we have the basis of the central modern debate: socialists see a managed, largely state-ordained economic framework with diminished room for private initiative, risk, or profitable reward; conservatives see the very order and freedom of society assisted in their necessarily government-influenced balance by dynamic forces of enterprise, profit, risk taking, and entrepreneurship. The neocon view, in contrast, embraces fragmentation, energizes economic and fundamentalist insurgence, and challenges the very right of democratically constituted societies to decide anything at all collectively for the common good. It is from this ideological platform that the real risks to order and freedom are launched. Neither the right to die in peace nor life-saving medical research is safe from this kind of insurgency.

When Benjamin Disraeli was first elected as a young MP in the United Kingdom, he joined other young MPs in a "One England" society that intuitively understood the existence of two nations in England, one wealthy and the other poor, disenfranchised, and without any prospects. He and his Tory colleagues became One Nation Conservatives, believing and advancing the premise that unless the suffering of the poor was diminished and their economic prospects increased, division and class war would cripple the United Kingdom. This movement launched what some have called the "progressive" and others the "populist" conservative tradition, which was very much part of Canadian conservative politics of the same era. Think of John A. Macdonald embedded in the Canadian political core. Think of, as part of this same tradition, R. B. Bennett, H. H. Stevens, John Bracken, John Diefenbaker, Bob Stanfield, Joe Clark, Brian Mulroney, Jean Charest, Bill Davis, Richard Hatfield, Peter Lougheed, and John Tory. In fact, the 2006 Harper campaign nodded in this direction in a host of ways, from universal tax cuts to increased support for health care.

From Disraeli to Churchill, from Macmillan to Heath, British conservatism, while shifting along the spectrum to the right and the left as economic and geopolitical realities required, has always been engaged in the thematic of nation and enterprise and the inexorable linkages between the two.

Until the advent of Preston Manning and the Reform movement in 1988, Canadian conservatism was very much in that mould. It shifted right and left to address excess on the left or right, but operated largely in the nation-building posture of Macdonald.

American postwar Republican presidents, such as Dwight Eisenhower, Richard Nixon, Gerald Ford, and George H. W. Bush, were very much in the more balanced American conservative tradition. Eisenhower worried about the military-industrial complex. Nixon actually engaged in social-welfare reform. And Bush sought to consolidate the post–Iron Curtain world order established by Ronald Reagan. Reagan conservatism was very much of the anti-state, anti-establishment variety, which, unburdened by any deep intellectual angst, became the perfect host for the neoliberal/neoconservative nostrums of the New York liberal refugees. It also embraced the religious, socially conservative right as necessary fellow travellers rather than as fragmenting vote spoilers. Add to this the frustration with President Carter's well-intended but apparent incompetence and the beginning in America and elsewhere of an identity-based, church-based pushback against the early forces of homogeneity launched by global market pressures, and you had the perfect storm by which moderate Republicans and Democrats would be overwhelmed by Reagan's revolution. The fact that Reagan was hail-fellow-well-met and a superb communicator assisted immensely. His conservatism was untraditional but never mean. He was a successful and humane politician doing for Republicans what Kennedy, in 1960, had done for Democrats. He was likeable and without guile, seemingly incapable of a mean or secret agenda. Thatcher and Mulroney were both helped by his momentum, and they helped that momentum themselves through strong multilateral engagement on defence, security, and trade policy.

There was, however, a serious difference among these three that is not often brought to the surface. Mulroney was not panicked by the role of the state. He had genuine anxieties about the apparatus he inherited from the Trudeau government and wanted to address clear excesses, such as the National Energy Program, which was perhaps one of the more confiscatory in Canadian public policy history. He did not, however, believe that all government was bad. In fact, on such issues as targeted family benefits, health care, national defence, Aboriginal self-government and land claims, he was prepared to use government to substantive and public benefit. He respected the broad reach and history of the Canadian public service, and aside from one or two symbolic changes, he not only left it intact but used some of its key and competent long-time players, such as David Dodge, Fred Gorbet, Derek Burney, Michael Sabia, Paul Tellier, Jocelyn Bourgogne, Suzanne Hurtubise, John Tate, and John de Chastelain, in vital and important roles central to Conservative government public-policy priorities. Consummate professionals, they and many like them served with balance, competence, and, where necessary, a pushback or two on substantive questions of implementation or policy design.

Margaret Thatcher had no compelling regard for the traditions and history of Whitehall or for the Oxbridge aristocracy of public men who had staffed the British public service over the years. She had the same disdain for the more moderate wing of her own party—the conservative tradition of Stanley Baldwin, Winston Churchill, Douglas Hume, and Ted Heath, who had sought to balance the needs of lower-income and unionized Britons with the larger economic and civil interests of the realm.

Reagan was elected and re-elected against Washington and its establishment, but he knew enough and was open enough to broad advice to put the equivalent of an American public-service Republican—George H. W. Bush—in the vice president's role. Bush had headed up the CIA, had served as U.S. ambassador to China, and was well connected to the diplomatic, defence, and intelligence community, who are a larger part of the U.S. public-service world than they are elsewhere. So while their common ground on trade policy and standing up to Soviet adventurism is often (and accurately) cited, the truth is that these were very different kinds of conservatives.

The nature of what conservatism has come to mean has been very much in flux since the end of the Cold War. The evaporation of the anchoring bipolar framework of two empires confronting each other produced new pressures and internal fissures in American conservatism, which contributed to debates and pressures among conservatives elsewhere.

Many thoughtful liberals may well suggest that the evaporation of the Cold War brought with it the evaporation of a large part of the necessary conservative world view. Conservatism is about boundaries, rules, principles, and values. It is about balance. The communist postwar threat, first recognized by Churchill while the Second World War was still being waged, was a signal pillar of modern conservative politics in all three countries—Canada, the UK, and the United States. Defence policy, foreign policy, domestic economic policy, and to some extent even social policy were all directly affected, in the three conservative parties, by the communist menace and the Soviet strategic threat—hence, the U.S. military buildup, support for Israel, tolerance for apartheid in South Africa, engagement in Vietnam, and hostility toward Cuba. Hence, for the UK, stronger defence priorities, a stronger alliance with the United States, and a conservative posture on the Middle East and South Africa.

Most notably in Canada, the Conservatives, from Diefenbaker on, became the first port of call and comfortable home of the many anti-communist refugees and immigrants from Eastern Europe, and also became the perpetual post-Diefenbaker proponents of stronger military relations and investment as part of Canada's NATO and NORAD alliance obligations. In the short period of 1962–63, a Conservative government split and then collapsed over the dynamics of this relationship, as it related to Diefenbaker's reticence to say "ready aye ready" to Kennedy during the Cuban Missile Crisis, to subsequent disagreements with the Americans and within the Canadian government over accepting nuclear warheads for Canada's Bomarc missiles, and to the division of opinion over what commitments had been made to the United States—and which ought to be kept.

All of which underscores the large void left when anti-communism and the Soviet threat become non-issues. The conservative world view very quickly became a philosophical framework that was not as concerned about ideological and totalitarian enemies outside the realm as about enemies of freedom and opportunity *inside* the realm.

I have always believed, about all three countries, that the absence of an external enemy could mean the absence of a conservative policy anchor. While Canadian conservatives were, before Mulroney, less focused on global commitments than their American and British counterparts, they could rally around the anti-Soviet cause with ease and relish.

The post–Cold War conservative world view became more concerned with fiscal balance, broad trade networks, and social organization within free societies. In the United Kingdom, the concern was with Europe and confronting the mix of stagflation and productive inefficiency associated with long periods of postwar Labour Party and "wet" Tory (conciliatory to big-labour) hegemony. In the United States, it was with the internal structure and organization of the American economy, its tax system, and its crime and social-value contexts. In Canada, it was with managing the internal east-west fault lines, made more challenging by language and the centralist/decentralist pressures in a country facing American protectionism.

The evaporation of the Cold War coincided in Canada roughly with the parliamentary approval of a free trade agreement with the United

States and a Conservative focus on tax reform (the GST) and on constitutional reconciliation. Mulroney's courage on these fronts was in some
measure economically transformational. But it also generated the predictable massive public recoil caused by any tampering with taxes and
by the neurotic nature of Canadians' relations with the United States. It
did not render Mulroney in 1993, after nearly a decade in government,
unviable, if viability means coming back as an opposition leader chas-
tened but unbowed and able to fight on, as other Conservative leaders
had done, including Macdonald, Diefenbaker, Meighen, and Clark. But
that viability was considered, by Mulroney and others, less viable after
two unprecedented, back-to-back majorities. The worry was that a new
Conservative mandate could not be won.

Thus Mulroney's decision, in 1993, to resign in the interests of the party,
undefeated. Structurally, as was the case with John Major's loss in the UK
and the defeat by Bill Clinton of Bush, this gave Canadian Conservatives
a unique and diverse legacy to absorb and engage.

So the end of the Cold War profoundly changed the makeup of the
conservative world view in all three countries. The belief in tradition, the
anxiety about undue rates of social change, and the desertion of steady
values of family, community, enterprise, and nation were still formally
in place, but they would be expressed differently as the full thrust of
the post–Cold War inheritance of Thatcher, Reagan, and Mulroney was
absorbed.

In the UK, Thatcherism became associated with an anxiety about the
European opportunity that had itself been engendered originally by
the Ted Heath wing of the Conservative Party. That anxiety would divide
the Tories between Eurocentric and Europhobic factions, ultimately toppling Mrs. Thatcher herself.

In the United States, Bush the father was toppled really from inside the GOP family by a Buchanan nativist wing that, while it could not win the nomination, could keep the Republicans from winning the election by dividing the convention that renominated President Bush while offending working mothers and ethnic minorities and starting a culture war that Americans never needed nor wanted.

And in Canada, the fault lines of the Mulroney coalition—Quebec nationalists and Prairie conservatives—fragmented after the success of free trade and from the oppressive impact of a deep and pervasive recession that made fresh, post-Meech constitutional negotiation of the Charlottetown Accord all but impossible. Mulroney's Herculean Charlottetown effort, which allowed Québécois and other Canadians to reject Charlottetown without literally tearing the country apart, and in which he was aided by such premiers as Bob Rae of Ontario, Joe Ghiz of Prince Edward Island, Robert Bourassa of Quebec, Roy Romanow of Saskatchewan, and Bill Bennett of BC, also dissipated his own personal political capital. Free trade, the GST, Meech Lake, Charlottetown—each had taken its toll, and the coalition had felt the strain. Much had been achieved by the Reagan/ Bush–Thatcher/Major–Mulroney conservative alliance, but the cost to the Conservative infrastructure in Canada was considerable.

These leaders left their societies stronger, more competitive, and more confident—very different from what they had found upon entering office. To a very real extent, aspects of their success, both good and bad, made each of their countries and electorates less in need of the kind of conservatism that they had each offered. Britain was economically stronger and more fiscally responsible; America had asserted a post–Cold War global presence through the first Gulf War that spoke of a better and more stable world; Canada had fixed historic trade access to the United States and had repositioned its tax system in concert with the more consumption-based premises of the OECD. This relative economic and strategic success in hand, as a result of the work of prior Conservatives, explains the ascendencies of Clinton, Blair, and Chrétien. But this geopolitical shift was not the only reason other kinds of contributions to Liberal hegemony become apparent when we assess the impact of Conservative divisions in Canada.

4

The Roots of Conservative Division

Reflecting on the historical and philosophical importance of division to Conservatives is like reflecting on the importance of water to fish. Division is the water within which conservatives and Conservatives swim.

I have experienced this from the beginning of my involvement with the party and the cause in my early teens. In 1962 and 1963, the Progressive Conservatives in government were divided over the nuclear weapons issue relative to our Bomarc anti-bomber missiles in Northern Quebec and in North Bay, Ontario. Doug Harkness, the defence minister, and others, including Léon Balcer and George Hees, came apart from Prime Minister Diefenbaker over the levels of alert and cooperation owed the Americans under President Kennedy during the Cuban Missile Crisis. These divisions, with American assistance, produced the almost-defeated minority Conservative government of 1962, down from a huge majority in 1958, and Pearson's first minority government of 1963. The divisions were reflective of a strong tendency within Conservative ranks to choose the honour of "policy differences honestly held" over the Liberals' more practical and more successful "unity over principle." Moreover, as Jeffrey Simpson so insightfully observed in his book *Discipline of Power* (1981), the public has every right to expect unity and coherence from a political party seeking the privilege of forming a government. If a party seeking to gain office or retain office is obviously not unified in purpose or coherent in position, what possible claim can it have on public confidence? Through strength of personality and unerring sensitivity to caucus and party personalities, Mulroney maintained a remarkable unity of purpose and team loyalty. Others were less successful.

This axiom very much played out in the local and national campaign, when I ran for Parliament in 1972 and 1974 for Robert Stanfield, in the riding of Ottawa Centre. In 1972, the Liberals ran an amazingly complacent and self-satisfied campaign under the rubric "The Land Is Strong." Our task under Stanfield's able and compassionate leadership was simple: point out where things could be improved in such matters as wasteful spending, unemployment, defence, housing, and federal-provincial relations. A coherent research-based campaign, the deployment of coordinated tour, speech content, and advertisements (all three very revolutionary at the time), and Stanfield's modest but determined assertion that there was "a better way" and that Canada "could do better" on so many fronts, helped propel the party from 75 seats to 105, with the Liberals reduced to 107 from 170.

Similarly, the NDP under David Lewis had advanced a coherent campaign against "corporate welfare bums," increasing their vote at Liberal expense. The Trudeau Liberal message was incoherent and unfocused. Trudeau was at his arrogant best, it seemed to me. As a novice candidate in Ottawa Centre, at the ripe old age of twenty-one, I moved the Conservatives to within 600 votes of the Liberals, who had held the riding by thousands for decades (the margin in this election was only 1,100 votes). The NDP came a close third, growing massively at local Liberal expense. The Conservatives seemed poised to form a government.

Just two years later, in 1974, the Liberals regained their majority, in large measure because we had little unity on a strong message relative to breaking the corrosive cycle of inflation (running at 8 per cent and up at the time). Stanfield and official party policy called for a ninety-day "freeze" on wages and prices to break the spiralling cycle. This cycle was putting immense pressure on rents, on seniors and veterans living on fixed incomes, and on businesses and farms, as well as on public-sector wage negotiations at all levels of government. This policy was especially important for seniors on fixed incomes. Wage earners, whose salaries are set for at least a year or two at a time, would not suffer from such a freeze, and at least the endless cycle of price increases would pause. Sadly, in Charlottetown during the 1974 campaign, former prime minister Diefenbaker enunciated a policy of price freezes without wage freezes; in Toronto, Jim Gillies, our finance critic, had his own quite different policy, as did Jack Horner in Alberta. Whatever else Trudeau was for or against, he was, throughout that campaign, against wage and price freezes of any kind. Not only did Liberals regain their majority in 1974, but they did so by making fun of the Tory policy—hence Trudeau's famous and devastating phrase, "Zap, you're frozen."

As the candidate in Ottawa Centre, I remember calling the boiler room at the Westbury Hotel in Toronto where Dalton Camp and Bill Grogan, aided by Wendy Cameron of the research office (soon to become Wendy Camp), were coordinating policy and speakers. Grogan and Camp were convinced that the public simply did not understand the simplicity of our message. "As a candidate who is knocking on doors from 9 a.m. to 9 p.m. every night, I have good news and bad news for you both," I pleaded. "They are understanding our messages on wage and price freezes . . . all our messages . . . That's the good news . . . The bad news? Well, they do not like any of it."

In a post-election seminar sponsored by *Reader's Digest* at Erindale College of the University of Toronto, Senator Keith Davey allowed that the Liberal victory was not so much the result of our party's wage and price control policy as of (as polling showed) the fact that different and incoherent policies on the same issue were coming from a Conservative Party purporting to be competent enough to govern. It's true that Trudeau brought in de facto controls some months later (with the Anti-Inflation Board and the 6 and 5 limits, which held public sector wages to a 6 per cent increase in one year, and 5 per cent the next, well beneath the wage settlement trend—highly inflationary—at the time). But that is essentially irrelevant to the issues of party coherence and campaign competence and of the perception and reality of unity. In my own riding, where I ran again in 1974, my able opponent, incumbent MP Hugh Poulin, would start all-candidates debates in this fashion: "I am delighted to debate Mr. Segal's party position on price and wage controls—I just don't know whether he will be defending Mr. Stanfield's or Mr. Diefenbaker's, Mr. Horner's or Mr. Gillies'!" That was extremely effective in a riding filled with young, mid-career, and retired public servants. I was able to increase the Conservative absolute vote over that of 1972, but only to lose by four thousand votes because the NDP vote was consumed by the Liberals. It made sense that swing voters would damn the apparent party of incoherence in 1974 by deserting the NDP for the Liberals.

On that election night—unlike on October 30, 1972, when it took until the early hours of the morning to declare a winner—CJOH, the local CTV affiliate, opened its coverage at 8:00 p.m. reporting the Liberals as gaining in the Maritimes and winning in Ottawa Centre. All the networks, having expected that I would win over the Liberal candidate in what they had identified as a swing riding, had set up cameras at the vacant former Loblaws store in the Glebe (on Bank Street South). My wonderful and creative campaign manager, Jerry Lampert, who now leads the BC Business Council in Vancouver but then was fresh out of Carleton University, called to say that, well, there was good news and bad news. The good news was that my vote was climbing steadily in all polls—and I would have had enough to have won in 1972. The bad news was that the NDP vote was collapsing in all polls to the Liberals' benefit, and my overall percentage of total votes cast was in rapid decline. He thought that I should get to the Loblaws from our suite at the Lord Elgin and concede quickly. My suggestion to him that I stand on a chair and tell the worst and most profane Lenny Bruce jokes I had ever heard was met with the stone-cold statement, "These are all the volunteers, who worked their hearts out—save the nastiness for the Grits."

He was, of course, quite right. But what happened to me happened in Ontario to an entire family of much better candidates, such as Ron Atkey in Toronto–St. Paul's, who were swept out to sea not because the policy was wrong, but because we had been incompetent and incoherent in how we defined and advanced it.

The next day, I had the most wonderful and funny call from Bob Stanfield.

"Well, young man," he said, "last night could have gone a little better . . ."

"Yes, sir," I agreed, "but I hope you will stay on as leader. There is still work for you to do."

"Well, I don't know about that, Hugh, but clearly we made a huge mistake."

"Wage and price controls, sir?" I asked.

"No, much more serious."

"What was that?"

"Letting Ontario into Confederation."

And with that reflection he ended the call.

It had been Ontario's vote shift that re-elected the Liberals. The west had stayed Tory!

During the minority Trudeau government of 1972–74, the Liberals had brought in the Foreign Investment Review Agency, had created the Crown-owned Petro-Canada, and had appeared to have absorbed much of the NDP policy platform. Voting Liberal in 1974 to prevent the risk of Conservative incoherence was rational for a plurality of voters in central Canada. Sound familiar?

Similar incoherence during the 1979–80 period, the brief Clark inter-regnum, also handed the Liberals an opportunity. As I have chronicled in my book *No Surrender*, it was Clark's inability to reconcile a series of unity issues, both in organization and policy, that produced the apparent incoherence set aside by Canadians in 1980 in favour of Trudeau. One of the key areas of division was the dispute on energy pricing between the Alberta Conservatives under Premier Lougheed and the Ontario Conservatives under Premier Davis. Clark, who as prime minister had failed to build a solid working relationship with either man, appeared unable or unlikely to find an acceptable balance between the producing and consuming provinces. In the end, this boosted the Liberal Party's polling numbers in Ontario and Quebec, making it irresistible for them to challenge John Crosbie's budgetary proposal in 1979–80 of an eighteen-cents-a-gallon levy.

Once again the fear of Tory incoherence made voting Liberal the rational thing to do. Once again Trudeau did the Conservatives one better, increasing the taxes on gasoline much more than we had proposed—showing that 1980, like 1974, was ultimately about competence and coherence, not about the policy itself.

Other Clark miscues in 1979, such as the Jerusalem embassy promise, the failure to reconcile with Claude Wagner in Quebec, and the long delay in actually beginning to govern, all added to the impression that Conservatives were either insufficiently prepared or insufficiently coherent for prime time. Being agendaless in Ottawa is simply suicidal. Sound familiar? It should to former prime minister Martin.

For Canadian conservatives, and for conservatives elsewhere, the real spectrum that matters is not that which defines left versus right or even libertarian versus social conservative. These are simply fragments of the larger spectrum, the one more essential to conservative and Conservative relevance, the spectrum defined by disunity at one end and coherence and unity at the other. And this has to do with more than just policy. It has to do with managing the cliques and associations related to different policy and regional interests and views; managing the intergenerational tensions that will always exist between different cadres within a political party; managing the leadership camps that dominate when new leaders are chosen; and managing and building one coherent organization with common goals and perceived interests.

From Sir John A. to Stephen Harper, this is the main precursor to success. Manage the incoherence well, and Canadians will vote Conservative. Fail to do so, and Canadians will vote Liberal, every time.

Canadian history is chock full of leaders who have been successful enough at this job one and those who have not. Why is it that, on the Conservative side, only Macdonald and Mulroney succeeded in both winning government and gaining back-to-back majorities? It is because these Conservative leaders used their larger-than-life personalities and intensity to reach out more broadly and convincingly to a broader spectrum of voters; because the force of their characters became an instrument with which to combat incoherence; because they used persuasive nation-building ideas to propel their party and governments. The virtuous circle of coherence—competence and unity in support of a plan, and a plan and set of ideas that require competence and coherence—was the key to seeking and gaining public support.

In the 1984 campaign, the Tories profited from Liberal incoherence, with John Turner vacillating between Bay Street and Trudeau left-liberal views of the country. In the 1984 campaign, Mulroney became the means of expression—on the right and the centre-left—of all grievances against Trudeau, from the excesses of the National Energy Program, the weakening of our Armed Forces, and the mismanagement of the Canada-U.S. relationship to the waste and overspending in Ottawa, the misrepresentation over the decade on everything from wage and price controls, and the gas tax. And, this time, the game Trudeau had played using the 1981–82 Constitution did not help in the swing provinces of Quebec and BC, and in any case, in Ontario and New Brunswick, Trudeau's constitutional allies, Davis and Hatfield, campaigned for Mulroney.

Mulroney shaped his majority as a nation-building, one-nation Tory.

Speaking to this Toryism were his subsequent policies and actions to bring Quebec back into the constitutional family, to negotiate historic agreements with the U.S. on acid rain and free trade, to commit to the western and Atlantic accords on energy to replace the excessive National Energy Program, and to establish new, locally rooted agencies on regional development—the Atlantic Canada Opportunities Agency in the Maritimes, the Federal Office of Regional Development in Quebec, and the Western Diversification Office in Alberta. All that, and Liberal campaign incompetence, went into his historic second majority victory.

In Canadian conservative history, both in Ottawa and the provinces, success on the spectrum of coherence has meant electoral success, and failure at coherence has produced electoral failure. Often the coherence of the recently campaigning became the incoherence of the newly elected, who could not manage in government—Diefenbaker and Clark being prime if well-meaning examples. A key period of risk always occurs when an administration and leader with focus and coherence are replaced by an administration and leader without much of either. Think of Camille Theriault in 1999 for the Liberals in New Brunswick, Kim Campbell in 1993 for the Conservatives federally, Frank Miller in 1985 for the Conservatives in Ontario, and John Turner in 1984 for the Liberals federally.

More recently, the inability of Liberals under Paul Martin to reconcile their own factions, integrate the Chrétienites, or make room for the John Manleys, Alan Rocks, and other possible future leadership contenders raised serious doubts about the coherence and balance of the Liberal offering. A similar incoherence had helped reduce Liberals to a minority in 2004, despite great and not unjustified expectations of how well Martin could be expected to do after he won the leadership in late 2003. Whether intended or not, the Liberals' approach to the Adscam problem—creating a wide-ranging and judicial inquiry as opposed to letting an independent police investigation go where the evidence justified—seemed motivated by a desire to settle scores within the Liberal Party. It reversed the general expectation, for a time, that Liberals had a monopoly on unity and Conservatives on fragmentation.

It is simply too facile to look only to the right/left divide within any political party as the sole source of this problem. All candidates for leadership represent a challenge to the existing balance, of which the policy and ideological mix is very much a part. Challenging from the right or the left is not in and of itself the problem; failing to integrate the diverse pieces once leadership is gained is the failure that counts. The more right-wing and anti-establishment Reagan understood this, bringing in as vice-presidential running mate George Bush, elder, who was very much part of the traditional Republican centre of noblesse oblige. Mulroney realized this when he appointed the pro-Clark Erik Nielsen as House leader when he won the leadership from Clark in 1983, and when he reached out to key organizers for the defeated leadership candidates such as Norman Atkins and Lowell Murray and gave them key election campaign roles. Mulroney owed his success to the fact that, though he himself was from Quebec, his campaign, policy, caucus, cabinet, and fundraising leadership were the best from all regions and factions of the party.

But Mulroney's success did not last, for the reasons discussed above, and we turn now to see what happened to Canadian Conservatives at the end of the Mulroney coalition in 1993, and why.

5

THE MULRONEY LEGACY

The real legacy of any leader or prime minister is determined by history.
We are still way too close to the end of Brian Mulroney's era to reflect accurately on the large forces that Mulroney both tamed and unleashed. And
as someone who was an active partisan and, for twenty months between
August 1991 and April 1993, a member of his staff, even the most generous historian could justifiably argue that I should be disqualified from
attempting a dispassionate account. But surely I should be allowed to look
at his legacy as a party politician in terms of what he inherited from Joe
Clark and what he left for leaders who would succeed him, as well as
to reflect on the implications of that partisan legacy for the Campbell,
Charest, and Clark years in the wilderness that ensued.

It is clear that Canada is a stronger, more fiscally stable, and economically more robust place than Mulroney inherited from prime ministers Trudeau and Turner because of the free trade agreement with the Americans, because of NAFTA, which brought in the Mexicans, because of the GST, and because of the many Aboriginal land claims settlements that took place under his leadership. Much of the value of Mulroney's work was less apparent during the recession of the late 1980s but bore verdant fiscal fruit for the Chrétien government. In a way, the managerial time and provincial cooperation essential for free trade and for the endless Meech Lake and Charlottetown negotiations made adopting the tough fiscal measures that Martin would employ under Chrétien impossible. (Imagine Mulroney cutting Bourassa's or McKenna's social transfers by one-third during the Charlottetown negotiations!) But what is more germane are the qualities of the party leader who brought the Conservatives out of the wilderness, and what forces were unleashed, wittingly or otherwise, by the Mulroney approach and leadership that shaped the dimensions of the partisan challenge to follow.

There are two kinds of leaders (and I have always thought this typology spans the left-right spectrum): directional and deliberative.

The directional leader does not have a to-do list every morning. This person may have a general sense of direction and some broad philosophical priorities and biases, but he or she is not a detail-focused actor in the process. Directional leaders may surround themselves with people of complementary skill sets, provided that the leaders are not themselves too insecure to retain people of real skill and compelling ability. The deliberative leader does have a list of specific goals to be achieved, and very precise interim and calibrated thresholds for achieving them. Bill Davis, for example, was very much a directional leader, whereas Peter Lougheed was extremely deliberative, with explicit, drill-down goals and subgoals in key areas of government.

What I don't think I understood about Mulroney when he won the leadership and took the party from the wilderness to a historic majority in 1984 was that he had made his own transition from directional to deliberative. Formative for him was his experience of losing the leadership in 1976 to Joe Clark and then winning that leadership in 1983, with all the necessary caucus destabilization of Clark after the Liberal victory of 1980. Mulroney, learning from 1976, became a leader for whom no broad strategic vision, no campaign plan, was any better than the critical and detailed implementation plans and efforts that backed it up.

Understanding the transition Mulroney made is essential to understanding his success and his unique legacy, and shines a spotlight on those who followed.

Being a child of the party since high school, Mulroney knew the networks, people, cliques, ambitions, anxieties, strengths, and weaknesses not only of his own wide swath of contemporaries, but also of a generation or so ahead of and behind his own. In the interregnum between 1976 and 1983, moving into the deeply detail-focused deliberative mode, he developed one of the finest political networks within the party, adding it to his already substantial journalistic and business networks.

The Michael Bliss or Peter C. Newman view of this may be that it was simply the cloying manifestation of an old Boston-style Irish pol (a putdown that Bliss especially liked). But this is unfair. Are they saying that it's now *de rigueur* for prospective prime ministers to wait for the country to come to *them?* Were Diefenbaker, Trudeau, Mackenzie King, Pearson, Martin, and Macdonald passive in support of their own ambition? Spare me. One of the greatest myopias of the endless Trudeaucentric cottage industry, which continues to be spawned by the CBC and others, is the notion that Trudeau did not conspire in his own ambition, that success was thrust upon him in 1967–68. After Trudeau's death came the myriad televised series, analyses, "life of" reels, a drama, and a novella—a season that seems to still be with us, so much so that I recently suggested to CBC president Robert Rabinovitch that he apply to the CRTC for a new network: "All Trudeau, All the Time"—an idea taken up by Stephen Harper at the National Press Gallery dinner in 2005. I suspect that the present campaign being orchestrated by or for Michael Ignatieff will, despite Ignatieff's many compelling qualities, embrace the same bogus mythology. Mythologies are always of some value, but the willing suspension of disbelief required to believe Trudeau's is almost too much to bear.

In fact, a democracy is in many ways better served when competitive political forces are replete with ambitious political activists who have that mix of public spirit, policy interest, and partisan entrepreneurship that defines the talent pool they offer Canadians locally, provincially, and nationally. There is significant evidence that, in good times and bad, when leaders come to power without any real experience in the vineyards, they lack the wherewithal to manage and lead. Mulroney did not suffer from that kind of deficit. Moreover, in both the 1984 and 1988 campaigns, and in the tight times before and after, it was that detailed deliberative anchor of Mulroney and his personality that kept the Conservative Party, the caucus, and the government viable.

That kind of leadership manifests itself in many ways, such as in being on the phone every night to party members, premiers, foreign leaders, and Canadian diplomats abroad, and in simply not being satisfied with someone else's summary reports. It meant walking into a room, a dinner, a rally, a Rotary lunch, and knowing half the people in the room—by name. It meant a pocket full of notes made at caucus every Wednesday morning, dealing with local riding issues—from casework to post office locations—and ensuring that they were followed up. It meant building relationships with premiers, caucus members, foreign leaders, and business and Aboriginal personalities, and doing so with substance, intellect, and compassion. It meant calling people not when they were on top, but when illness, misfortune, or the vicissitudes of life had them on a bit of a slide.

I remember one call from the prime minister in early 1993, at the end of the day, in which he cheerfully asked how my day had gone. My report included a telephone call from an Atlantic premier, a meeting of a committee I was chairing with Finance and Health Canada on a guaranteed annual income, and a throne speech planning session, all of which struck me as an honest day's work. "Well," the prime minister retorted, with more than a little irritation, "one of our MPs just had a car accident with his wife, and she has a badly broken arm, and it is your job, beyond all the policy and planning, to make sure I hear about that right away! So get your priorities straight." It was the only time the prime minister ever trained his temper on me. His point was clear: without caucus cohesion, unity, and loyalty, nothing else mattered.

And it was endless. No Conservative was too remote, no labour leader was too far to the left, no Aboriginal leader too angry or alienated for Mulroney to call. When Clark was leader, both between 1976 and 1983 and after 1998, almost no one ever merited a call. Mulroney's style of leadership would see major speeches drafted sixteen or seventeen times until he was happy with them. His style of leadership meant that five or six legal suitcases of homework accompanied him home to 24 Sussex nightly, with a broad range of foreign and domestic issues—along with correspondence from mayors, union locals, foreign leaders, and diplomatic dispatches from our own embassies abroad—for his personal review. He was as engaged intellectually in the policy of government as Trudeau was, but unlike the latter, he would place many calls every night outside the Ottawa bubble, to benefit from advice, sentiments, perceptions, and perspectives not always available from the PMO or the PCO. And it was in that mix that he kept his balance, and that of his government. Mulroney was also substantially more collegial than most leaders. He actually had and encouraged strong ministers who had clout, who had real authority, and who thereby helped him sustain both balance and coherence. Among them were Don Mazankowski, John Crosbie, Mike Wilson, Joe Clark, Kim Campbell, Barbara McDougall, Bill McKnight, first Lucien and then Benoît Bouchard, Bernard Valcourt, and Elmer MacKay. For all of Mulroney's focus on controlling the party's levers of power (and Clark's inability to do so, which was destructive for a generation), he was always secure enough to encourage his ministers to be strong ministers—clearly a trait with which Paul Martin could never get comfortable, to mention only one prime minister who was insecure on this point.

Mulroney's massively personal and extroverted leadership style—his high-touch dynamic—was in stark contrast to the little-touch-as-possible approach Clark had embraced. At the end of the successful 1979 election campaign, when Clark and the Progressive Conservatives beat the "unbeatable" Trudeau, Clark's volunteer advance team sent several hundred photos for him to sign, thanking the many volunteers who had helped during the campaign. Over the many weeks during which the photos were not signed, it became apparent that the leader was simply not comfortable with numbers of people having signed thank-you photos of the prime minister on their walls. To be fair, one could often sense a concern on Clark's part that no group, individual, or MP should be perceived to have undue influence. Unfortunately, however, this could also produce a reality in which no one beyond the leader had any real stake in his success. Some day Clark's memoirs may enlighten us on this discomfort with the core human contact absolutely vital to the modern leadership of a political party. In the end, it ended his leadership of the Conservatives in 1983, even though the party was over 50 per cent in the polls.

But the problem for the party when Mulroney resigned in 1993 was that it was hooked on the high-touch leader who made reaching out a *sine qua non* of leading. And while Mulroney had his weaknesses—neither humility nor uncertainty could ever compete with his determination and, on occasion, hubris—I would argue that even these weaknesses were largely put to work in the interest of the country first and the party second. I know for a fact that after the Meech Lake setback, his priorities were first to move the planned October 1992 Quebec referendum away from independence and back to a much lower-risk constitutional proposal, then to sort through NAFTA, then to address the party's needs, and, only after that, to reflect on his own future. (Those were the terms of reference under which he asked me to join the PMO in 1991. It was a position from which he never wavered.)

But whatever his weaknesses, they were balanced by the undeniable drill-down skills he brought to the party. In a sense, the Conservative Party was spoiled, and it would not know how much it was spoiled till its leadership changed in the spring of 1993.

Another secret to Mulroney's leadership and to Conservative success under his leadership was the coalescence of disparate forces—the unique national coalition he had shaped in the party and in the country. Its structure and counterweights were fundamental to Conservative success under him; their evaporation would be as fundamental to the party's electoral collapse.

Too much has been made, in my view, of the so-called alliance with Quebec sovereigntists. Those who advance this view fail to understand the roots of the Conservative Party in Quebec. There, the party died as a separate provincial force when the Union Nationale was formed, from left-wing liberals and nationalist conservatives who were opposed to the private hydro monopolies. That movement, which was populist and anti-business, was also nationalist. The victory that swept the Union Nationale to power was based on a strong pro-Quebec, Ottawa-wary stance. This remained the party's stance throughout its history, under Paul Sauvé and Daniel Johnson, Sr. The Union Nationale party that supported Diefenbaker in 1957 and 1958 was based on the premise, "*coopération toujours, assimilation jamais!*" Their goal was never to take Quebec out of Canada but to have the tools to protect the French-language culture and civilization in a Quebec built firmly into the confederal bargain. It is not the least surprising that after Trudeau's immense centralization, the brutalizing referendum, the constitutional isolation of Quebec (more, in my view, the fault of Lévesque and the PQ than of Trudeau, to be fair), nationalists would prefer a Mulroney government with a Quebec-based leader who had been part of the Union Nationale infrastructure for years.

Furthermore, it was clear that the coalition could take shape because there was no contradiction between it and Alberta's desire to unravel the confiscatory National Energy Program; or Bay Street's desire to reduce taxes and stop the burgeoning growth of the federal government; or Conservative interest in a more robust defence and foreign policy, less churlish than Trudeau's and more reflective of the commonly held values of NATO, our allies, and Canada's traditional friends; or Atlantic Canadians' feelings of being left out of the decisions that mattered. Mulroney had the legitimate regional roots and associations and the coalition to make it happen. Those who saw in the Mulroney candidacy something to inspire hope and opportunity included small-c conservatives in Alberta, small-town Ontario farmers, Red Tories from the big cities, decentralists and nationalists in Quebec, and Atlantic Canadians who wanted more regional economic decisions made closer to home. These were not bedfellows without common cause: it was a coalition of Canadians who had felt, quite accurately, that they were outside the charmed Liberal establishment circle of Ottawa, which had appeared under Trudeau from 1980 to 1984 to become more aloof, more remote, deeply wasteful, more self-reverential, more unaffordable, and less rooted in the Canada that Canadians actually knew. Trudeau's final "peace tour," while no doubt well intentioned, seemed in the end to focus more on Trudeau than on Canada or Canadians. While they were unfailingly polite about it, world leaders did not appear to understand much of it at all.

In 1993, Mulroney's departure had to mean the end of his coalition. Speaking to the range of his appeal, to the manifest loyalty he sustained (even when he was down to single digits in the polls), and to the complexity of his coalition was the fact that I had been happy to support the same leader as did David Frum—that Benoît Bouchard, Walter McLean, David MacDonald, and Dalton Camp could support the same leader as Gordon Walker, Len Gustafson, Rod Love, and Mike Harris. And keep in mind that many of us had not supported him in either of his leaderships (I was for Claude Wagner in 1976 and for Clark in 1983).

Forming a new coalition would be the first task of the Mulroney's successor. It would not be easy.

6

The Campbell Interlude

February 24: Prime Minister Mulroney announces his resignation as Canada's eighteenth prime minister.

June 13: Kim Campbell is sworn in as Canada's nineteenth prime minister and the first woman ever to hold that office.

October 25: The Liberal Party of Canada wins a majority government, with 178 seats. The Progressive Conservatives are reduced from 154 to 2. The Reform Party, led by Preston Manning, wins 52 seats. The Bloc Québécois, led by Lucien Bouchard, wins 54 seats and becomes the official opposition.

Seven months in 1993 saw a historic second Conservative majority government not only be defeated by the Chrétien Liberals, but be crushed by *three* parties beyond all recognition. Partisans of Kim Campbell, such as David McLaughlin, in his 1994 book on her, would argue that she had received a "poisoned chalice" about which nothing could have been done. Many Mulroney loyalists argued that the defeat was due to a series of profound misjudgments made by Campbell and her team, from the moment she won the leadership.

The hard truth is that some of the seeds of defeat were sown long before Campbell declared for the leadership. In fact, party pollster Allan Gregg had shared some fundamental findings on this front at the first general meeting of the party after the successful free trade election of 1988. That was an election in which the provinces of Quebec and Alberta combined with swing seats in Atlantic Canada, British Columbia, and Ontario to put the Conservatives over the top. Underneath this historic win, which allowed Parliament to approve the Canada-U.S. Free Trade Agreement—perhaps one of the most historic wins in any Canadian electoral battle—a clear and determined shift in the structure of the Conservative coalition was forming up.

Assembling a coalition of voters is the primary duty of a campaigning politician, leader, or party. Elements of the coalition may break off, and new elements may join, and as a result, tending to a coalition between elections is one of the great balancing acts of any government and prime minister. Not every decision made in the public interest will please all parts of one's coalition. Tilting toward full funding for Catholic schools in Ontario was not helpful to the Ontario Tory coalition of 1985; inability to reconcile Alberta and Ontario energy price conflicts in 1979–80 fractured Clark's fragile coalition of voters in Ontario; inability to sustain a coherent sense of direction fractured the urban part of the Conservative coalition inherited by Ernie Eves from Mike Harris.

This coalition imperative is made more challenging by the need to broaden the tent and ensure opportunities for coalition growth. Here the debate quickly becomes centred on a trade-off between new converts and those who may leave for various reasons.

The 1988 election results were a sea change in the usual structure of the Tory coalition. In the first election I contested as a candidate for Stanfield in 1972, and in most subsequent elections, the core Tory coalition consisted of bedrock Tory voters—usually male, Protestant, from small towns, over forty, and with less than a college education. Added to this, depending on the dynamics of policy, leaders, advertising, and one's opponents' follies, would be Conservative/Liberal switch voters, urban or suburban, in Ontario; some young people in the cities; and some NDP/Conservative switch voters in BC or Saskatchewan. Key areas since Diefenbaker's 1957–63 government, such as the Prairies, western cities, and largely old Orange eastern Ontario (from Cornwall to the Durhams and up through Simcoe and Parry Sound), would largely stay Conservative. On occasion, urban breakthroughs in the Etobicokes and the Don Valley Easts and the Scarboroughs would add to the mix and portend a close election result.

The popular notion that these were all wealthy voters was simply untrue—witness the work done by Queen's University's George Perlin, Allan Gregg, and the *Globe and Mail*'s Patrick Martin in a 1980s study of the family income of those who attend Liberal, NDP, and Conservative conventions. Perlin, Gregg, and Martin found that Conservatives had by far the lowest family income of the three. This was partly because urban Liberals had more two-income households, as was the case with the NDP. And it was partly because there were often more farm families in the Tory party, families that classically have less declarable income than salaried, city-based, two-earner households. When Conservatives depended on their base, it was not (some parts of Rosedale, Calgary, and Point Grey notwithstanding) overpopulated with the wealthy and well educated. In places like Atlantic Canada, Newfoundland, rural eastern Ontario, and, when fortunate, rural *Québec profond,* the economic makeup of the Tory voter was anything but wealthy. And that was true whether those voters chose the Tories because their parents had, because the Tories had long since been the "Orange" or more provincialist party, because of the British connection, or because of the anti-communist connection (for Canadians from Eastern Europe in large parts of west Toronto, and in the Prairies).

The point that Gregg made when he briefed the Conservative Party after the 1988 election was that the ground had shifted. In many parts of the old Tory core areas, there had been a shift of the old core. Yes, they had been replaced by new, wealthier, better-educated urban switch voters who felt confident about their own prospects under free trade. But swing voters are just that: they can swing toward or away from a party based on the issues and circumstances of the time. The bedrock Tory voters had fragmented in some parts of the country. Ridings like Leeds-Grenville, Kingston and the Islands, and Ottawa West and ridings in Saskatoon, Nova Scotia, Newfoundland, Prince Edward Island, and New Brunswick swung Liberal, doubling Turner's seats from forty to eighty. Normally, there would have been a rural, small-town, older demographic to the Tory vote.

The 1988 election changed all that. The dynamics of this free trade election produced some fascinating political trade between Liberals and Conservatives. Traditionally, better-educated, wealthier, young professional Canadians usually voted Liberal. After all, it was the business-establishment party, with its strong (if self-proclaimed) managerial record in the federal government. It had won the vast majority of elections at that level, had handed out the vast majority of largesse, and was the place to be for those building their professional and business careers. I would often joke on *Canada AM* that Senator Michael Kirby, the panellist for the Liberal Party on that program's pundits panel, claimed to have "fundamental hard-core principles." But, I would add, "if you don't like those, he has others . . ." The truth behind this line was that Liberals were seen to be more easily adaptive and certainly less rigid. They were, in addressing the managerial task of running the government, substantially less burdened by ideological or policy conviction. Generally speaking, that kind of flexibility is attractive—or, it *was* attractive in the Trudeau years. And for any profoundly non-partisan urban voter, this was especially appealing. Keep in mind that fewer than 3 per cent of Canadians have ever held any party card.

In the 1988 election, many of the wealthiest, most urbane, and best-educated voters chose the Conservatives and free trade. Unbelievably, Liberal ridings such as Outremont in Montreal went Conservative. Some of the nastiest anti–free trade demonstrations in the entire campaign were held in quiet, unassuming Kingston, where Flora MacDonald, despite her personal popularity, was defeated by the now Speaker of the House, Peter Milliken, a competent local lawyer whose father was a well-liked cardiologist. All across the country, Tories would lose rural seats only to pick up urban seats in their place. Ethnic Toronto turned to the Liberals, but better-educated and wealthier parts of the city, ethnic or not, turned to the Tories. In 1988, the Tories had declined from 211 seats to 154.

The importance of this switch was both policy-based and largely proportional relative to the coming challenge. Bedrock Tory ridings—those that always stayed Tory—in the worst of elections so far had, in considerable measure, defected to the Liberals on issues such as milk marketing board preservation, abortion, and bilingualism. In many ridings, smaller parties such as Christian Heritage or Family Coalition opposed free trade, bilingualism, and abortion, and spun off just enough Tory votes to elect the Liberals. In the west, Preston Manning's Reform Party picked up sizeable votes without seats but set down an impressive base. In other ridings, the public-sector unions' anti–free trade campaign helped the Liberals far more than the NDP. And while Ontario held, it was Alberta and Quebec that saved the Tories. On election night, Bill Fox, Mulroney's former director of communications and a former Ottawa and Washington bureau chief for the *Toronto Star*, sat on a CTV panel with me watching the early, devastating results from the Atlantic region, where the Liberals were surging to a quick lead. I don't think either of us exhaled until the polls closed in Quebec and the flood of Tory seats arrived on the screen.

The problem with this new Tory coalition was that while it produced a historically unprecedented second Tory majority, it could not, by definition, be as permanent or dependable as the one it replaced. Allan Gregg made the case on this "fragility" for all to hear. These new Tory voters had previously been somewhere else. They were voting for free trade because the economy was doing well, and so were they. They felt confident about their capacity to compete and, more importantly, about Canada's capacity to win. History has proven them and the policy profoundly right. But history would not protect Kim Campbell.

By definition, these voters would require continued solid economic prospects to keep them in the coalition. And those who were strong supporters in Quebec were also there because the Meech Lake Accord, which Mulroney and the provinces, including Quebec, had negotiated in the first term, was very much alive and, for all intents and purposes, quite well. This historic accord, which had brought Quebec back into the constitutional consensus it had chosen not to be part of under the Lévesque–Morin–Parizeau sovereigntist government in power in 1982, was a rallying point of cohesion that cemented moderate nationalists, reasonable federalists, and pro-free trade business forces together in Quebec, in support of re-electing a Mulroney government.

Campbell—or, for that matter, the Conservative Party—cannot be blamed for the deep recession that hit large parts of the free world in 1989–93, for the collapse of the Meech Lake Accord in the legislatures of Newfoundland and Manitoba in 1990, for the massive animosity toward the GST, or for the rise of the Canadian dollar to near ninety cents. But the effect of all this was inevitable. In a sense, symbolic of the coalition's fragility was the departure of Lucien Bouchard as part of the Meech Lake debacle, even though it may have been part of a long-term plan on Bouchard's part to advance his own political options as a sovereigntist leader. The year 1988 also saw an increase in Preston Manning's Reform Party vote in many parts of the west. In fact, I have always believed that without free trade in the west, and especially Alberta, Manning might well have picked up almost enough seats to form an official party in the House of Commons. That he did not speaks to the intensity of Mulroney's campaigning and to the undeniable support for free trade in Alberta. But to the west Manning had become the real opposition. And when the irrepressible Deborah Grey became the first Reform Party member of the House in a by-election soon after the 1988 election, the war of attrition had begun, with the western Tory core as the target.

The dynamic in the Conservative Party that saw Campbell chosen as the party's next leader reveals a great deal about the level of denial alive and well in the post-Mulroney-resignation, pre-convention time frame. Mulroney has always claimed—and I have always believed—that his first wish was for a hotly contested leadership fight between Ontario's Mike Wilson and Barbara McDougall, Quebec's Jean Charest, the Atlantic's Bernard Valcourt, and BC's Kim Campbell, along with one or two others. This was something that his final cabinet shuffle tried to promote, with McDougall moving to Foreign Affairs, Campbell to Defence, Wilson to Trade, and so on. The truth of the matter, however, is that large parts of the party apparatus felt they had been signalled that Campbell was his favourite. She was young; she was from British Columbia; she was of the boomer generation (the early wave). She was not part of the hoary pre-1983 Tory past—in fact, she had not formally been a Conservative for very long at all. I supported Charest for leader, after I left the PMO on April 30, 1993, and after the odds-on favourite campaign wagon had pushed key contenders out after or even before declaring. I and others who supported Charest did so not because we were sure he could *win* an election, but because we were sure he could lead us in a difficult election, one in which our coalition would be under severe attack. We knew he was a prodigious campaigner, had deep Conservative and Union Nationale roots in Quebec, and had the kind of easy and fluid bilingualism that put both language groups in the country completely at ease. Our problem with Campbell was not her intellect, engagement, purpose, or dedication. We simply did not believe she had the roots in the Tory party and enough remaining coalition fragments to keep the party whole when the going got really rough.

My support for Charest emerged, basically, from two compelling sources. First and foremost, while I liked Kim Campbell and felt she had immense qualities, I was convinced by various events that she lacked the seasoning to lead the party. I saw this when Campbell and her BC caucus colleagues succeeded in winning a battle within the government over science funding, choosing a large "big science" multi-hundred-million-dollar project at UBC (KAON) over a smaller multi-project approach across Canada, advanced by the then science minister William Winegard, the MP for Guelph and former president of the University of Guelph. Campbell chose, rather than to be gracious in victory, to be demeaning and triumphal. To understand how shallow her roots were in the party, you need only to have looked at the faces of Ontario ministers and caucus as she, having already had the prime minister choose her position over Bill's, rhetorically drove a bulldozer over Bill's face. Bill was professional, courteous, and loyal to the end. Hers were not the sensitivity or judgment or team skills required to combat the Liberal-Reform-Bloc onslaught that the Tories would face. At the convention in the late spring of 1993, she was unable even to excite her own supporters.

Charest, on the other hand, was not only a scrapper, but someone who understood the dynamics of the party's base. CityTV held a debate on free trade, with the Tory team headed up by Charest. This was between the 1987 provincial election in Ontario, where Ontario Tory leader Larry Grossman's steadfast support of Mulroney on free trade helped the ever-opportunistic David Peterson win a historic landslide (reducing the Tories from 58 to 16 seats) and the actual federal election of 1988. Charest was magnificent. To an audience that was young and not terribly political but quite edgy, he made a coherent and solid case. He truly carried the debate and the day. The phone-in poll that followed was just about a dead heat between the pro– and anti–free trade vote. This was a historic rhetorical hill taken in massively Liberal and very anti–free trade Toronto and Ontario—just as the federal election season was to get underway.

Watching his facility, sincerity, and fluidity, the ease with which he connected with a younger generation—and knowing of his roots and Tory/Union Nationale sensibilities—I sensed then that Jean Charest was the real thing.

The likelihood of a Conservative victory in 1993 under any leader, including Mulroney—after the Meech Lake collapse, the Charlottetown referendum defeat, a debilitating recession, the ongoing opposition to free trade, and the drop in the polls to 9 per cent for the government when it brought in the hated GST—was so exceedingly slim that to blame Kim Campbell alone for the depth of her defeat is to simply rewrite history on the premise of malicious scapegoating. (I used to remind ministers in cabinet that there were more Canadians who thought Elvis Presley was alive than Canadians who planned to vote for us, to which Bill McKnight of Saskatchewan, a superb minister of defence, would counter, "They may be the same people.") Charest would also have lost that election, but his loss would have looked no worse than Prime Minister Turner's in 1984 (40 Liberal seats) and might even have looked like Turner's results in 1988 (80 seats).

But the profound wilderness experience of the two-seat result in 1993 could well have been avoided. The Tories would have been the government in waiting, and we could have avoided a decade of wilderness, the fragmentation of conservative forces, and the complete almost decade-long absence of conservative contribution to the national policy debate.

Much has been said about the 1993 campaign. The perspective of a decade offers some further opportunity for insight. Campbell cannot be blamed for "not knowing what she didn't know," as Senator Lowell Murray, a strong supporter of hers, used to say post-election. She was the instrument the party chose to avoid confronting both its own history and public antipathy to its unpopular policies and to its unpopular outgoing leader. The public antipathy was sidelined for a time, but it never disappeared.

While there was a period during which Campbell was the most popular prime minister in Canadian history, in the end inexperience would provide more pitfalls than novelty could generate momentum. Seriously destabilizing to the electorate were matters from personal pacing to debate strategy to an unfathomable statement on what is or is not appropriate to discuss during an election campaign to the decision to withdraw a controversial ad. And that is not to mention her lack of experience and her lack of deep roots in the conservative communities and the conservative family. But the election was lost for reasons beyond her control, likely before it began. That it was lost so badly was because she lacked the capacity to control the dimensions of the loss through a strategic adjustment to save the furniture and base. Such a tactical manoeuvre is a very tough one for the most experienced leader. But even a rusty old politician like Turner had found a way to do it in 1984.

The way in which the coalition came apart—in a sense creating a vacuum on the right, as opposed to a simple defeat—contributed directly to the fragmented competition between players on the right. That competition would weaken and diminish the centre-right of Canadian politics outside the Liberal Party. It would also help create room for the centre-right *within* the Liberal Party, an opportunity a deficit-fighting Paul Martin would ultimately successfully exploit.

The likelihood of any coalescence on the right was almost impossible, given the degree to which the Campbell-Conservative disintegration was accelerated by the vitriolic nature of Manning's anti-Mulroney, anti–Conservative Party strategy (not hard to understand from Manning's perspective) and the extent to which that strategy could be seen by traditional Tories as anti-French, anti-immigration, and anti-diversity (whether or not that was Manning's intent). Manning may genuinely believe that this was never his intent, purport, or tactic, but the 1997 ads that ran a line through a host of French-Canadian leaders' faces may have fixed some contempt or even hatred in the minds of many for many years to come.

Because conservatives in general and Canadian Conservatives in particular are less prone to big-government centralizing solutions and partial to more local and provincial jurisdiction (or even just to respecting the division of powers in our constitution), their fate is tied to local political organizations. Whatever hierarchy of Ottawa-centred apparatchiks federal Liberals depended on, Tories drew their strength and sustenance (especially during the long periods of Liberal federal government) from the provinces. In almost every province (except BC and Quebec, which both lacked competitive provincial Conservative parties), the organizations of the federal and provincial Tory parties were essentially made up of the same people, which meant that the risk of an unbridled regionalism, of the kind Manning launched, threatened the very survival of the Tories. It is not surprising that Tory premiers Gary Filmon of Manitoba, Ralph Klein of Alberta, and even Mike Harris of Ontario sought early ententes cordiales with Manning and his people. Fragmentation of the federal PC forces was one thing, but any premier who let that contagion infect his provincial team would simply have been organizationally derelict. So Manning not only attacked the Tory federal base but also, by building de facto non-aggression pacts with provincial Tory premiers, made the Tories less than enthusiastic supporters of the federal leader *du jour*, which in post-1993 Canada meant Charest.

The critical historical issue after the 1993 election, especially in terms of the decade to come, was the extent to which the nature of Campbell's time as leader had a formative impact on the dynamics of fragmentation—the wilderness reality that Canadian conservatives would have to face. The hard truth is that a simple Liberal victory of substance would have been temporary and, with hard work, reversible. But the extent to which Campbell lost hold of the entire coalition, as opposed to simply parts of it, meant that the factors shaping the conservative wilderness would be mutually reinforced by ideological and regional tensions. These were the tensions that Mulroney had buried better than almost any Conservative leader. Others, such as Bob Stanfield and Joe Clark, had managed them at least to the point of keeping the Conservative Party a viable and potentially victorious national alternative.

Campbell was thrust into a crucible for which she was not ready. To some extent, being a newly joined-up Conservative (as of 1988), she could not have known how intense the centrifugal pressures could be. The long-time Conservatives who did support her seemed detached from the larger history and perpetual fragility of the Conservative coalition. And in the fragmentation their choice and decisions helped cause, they became, unwittingly, the very best purveyors of that very Tory disintegration for which Reform and Liberals had hoped and planned.

Two days after the election, in which only Jean Charest in Sherbrooke and Elsie Wayne in Saint John had been elected for the Conservative Party, I returned to Kingston, after having been the Tory on CBC TV's election-night coverage. Both Heather Reisman, the Liberal panellist, and Stephen Lewis, the NDP panellist, had been kinder and more gentle than I deserved. It was by no means clear that election night was more than a wild aberration. A decade-long dilution of the Conservative voice in Canada was neither expected nor predicted.

My wife, Donna, and I went out to Chez Piggy, a wonderful neighbourhood restaurant in downtown Kingston owned and operated by (the now late) Zal Yanofsky, formerly of the Lovin' Spoonful and a local personality of standing and of an over-the-top sense of humour. As Donna and I stood at the maître d's desk waiting to be led to a table, Zal, coming down the stairs by the bar, saw us and bellowed at the top of his lungs, "Segal . . . party of two!"

As our fellow patrons collapsed in laughter, Donna and I good-naturedly wound our way to our table. As we sat down, it occurred to me that here, in the first capital of the Province of Canada, Sir John A.'s hometown, the devastation of the parliamentary party had been just about total.

Fortunately, hemlock was not on the menu.

7

The Charest Resurgence

From late fall of 1993 to April of 1998, when Jean Charest had effective control of the Progressive Conservative Party, the challenges to party success were spread liberally around. The departure of Kim Campbell, which was about as civilized as a party so broadly crushed could sustain, facilitated Charest's elevation by broad demand within the party. All those who had contested against Campbell in the 1993 leadership offered Charest support and vows of loyalty. His personal charisma, depth within the party, and easy facility with the media—and the fact that, along with Elsie Wayne of Saint John, New Brunswick, he held half the Tory seats in the Commons—made him the obvious choice. He had not been chosen in an open convention, but was endorsed by a party-wide delegate convention in Hull in 1994, a vote that was essentially unanimous.

Charest had the party at his side and a strong popular desire for him to make the party a contender again. His challenge, however, was dominated by three compelling burdens: a huge party debt inherited from the Campbell interregnum, a divided Conservative cause in Ontario and the west, and a crushing Conservative consensus that democratizing the party's internal structure was vital to rebuilding. Of these burdens, the first two meant trouble right away and the last meant trouble over time.

Charest himself symbolized some of the best of what Conservative prospects might be. He got on well with the west's Ralph Klein and the Atlantic's Tories. Bay Street liked him, even if he was perceived as not as determined as he might be on lowering taxes. He got on easily with the Senate caucus, a relationship bolstered by his strong association with long-time leaders such as John Lynch-Staunton, Marjorie LeBreton, and Norman Atkins. He encouraged bright young hard-working Conservatives such as Dr. Kellie Leitch (from Alberta and Ontario), Graham Fox (from francophone Ontario), and Alexander Grieve (from Niagara and Toronto) to take major riding, organizational, and policy roles in the party. He reached out and inspired young Conservative activists like Stella Cicollini from Brampton, Chris Bradley from Peel, Jamie Bailie in Nova Scotia, Martha Ellis in Prince Edward Island, and Byng Giraud and Alex Kenyan in British Columbia. Conservatives of standing and substance in Newfoundland, such as Lynn Verge and Loyola Hearn, were also important parts of the primal base that was supportive of Charest. Young Quebeckers like Dany Renauld, a bright, thoughtful, and capable marketing strategist, and André Bachand, a mayor from the Shefford-Asbestos region, were all strong parts of Charest's new guard. He kept contact with younger Conservatives who had run in 1993, or who would run in 1997—people who were to shape a Tory renewal in the future, such as Peter MacKay in Nova Scotia, and Mayor Rick Borotsik of Brandon, Manitoba.

In the area of party finances, Charest left Don McDougall of London and the indefatigable Irving Gerstein of Toronto very much in charge. While McDougall did not stay for more than a year (and departed essentially because the forces of party democratization made the fundraising and management process more difficult), regular large fundraisers and dinners, combined with direct mail support, managed to keep the party afloat. This flotation (despite the huge debt) was a tribute to Gerstein's determination, hard work, and nimbleness with the banks—and to the banks' desire not to be responsible for shutting the Tories down.

Charest contributed to this viability in many ways that are to his lasting credit. The imperial leadership of the old days was gone. Party HQ staff was pared back massively. Charest himself would travel on donated frequent flyer points and, where feasible, by bus (not a chartered bus, but a regularly scheduled intercity bus), or in borrowed or rented cars. He would stay in supporters' homes to save money. Frugality, a young and committed staff (policy advisers such as Graham Fox, party organizers such as Roxanne Benoit and national party president Pierre Fortier), and his own enthusiasm and hard work combined to energize many young people and traditional supporters. Across the country, young and able conservatives—such as Sarah Poole in Rosedale, Peter Atkins in St. Paul's, and Mark McQueen on Bay Street—engaged to help. Charest's superior capacities in front of a camera, at a podium, and in the House also helped immensely.

Charest's struggle to revive the party came at a time of a newly prominent Reform Party under Preston Manning, which, from a fifty-plus caucus and with funds coming in from both the oil patch and street level across the west, was enjoying a geographically limited but still remarkable surge. The party had almost attained official opposition status from a one-seat start before the 1993 election. As well, Charest faced the Lucien Bouchard–led official opposition in Ottawa, a Bloc Québécois made up of some of the soft nationalist colleagues he had known as Conservative supporters throughout the 1980s.

Charest decided to essentially give in to the apparatchik view of what the core evils facing the Conservative Party really were. It was the only way to manage all these pressures—including those in the west and in southern Ontario, where many provincial Conservatives were very much for joining the two conservative parties together.

This view, expressed by sincere and hard-working party activists such as Ontario party president Peter Van Loan, could be summarized in this manner: the massive defeat of the Conservatives in 1993 was really the result of a top-down elite who were not truly accountable to the rank and file. Only through true grassroots accountability could this kind of setback be avoided in the future.

This is, of course, the great populist myth usually embraced by parties that are out of power. Like any myth, it is not without some merit and some truth. But like all myths, there is far less to the underlying reality than meets the eye. This myth had, in 1994–95, two significant attractions. First, it was populist, and as such seemed a democratic response to the endemic and likely cosmetic populism of Manning's Reform Party. (This was one of Manning's greatest camouflage initiatives: his party was ruthlessly top-down in management but had created the sense of populism and of being bottom-up that took in both the media and its own rank and file.) Second, it was a way of saying that whoever was to blame for the debacle of 1993, it was not the rank-and-file membership of the Conservative Party, who had voted for Campbell. This was surely an opportune and self-preserving stance for Charest to take. It was, in a sense, the path of least resistance, one further way to ensure cohesion and loyalty until the 1997 election.

The reasoning in these sorts of circumstances is always the same: buy peace till the next election; if it goes well, the future is bright for the leader; if it doesn't, well, there is no future anyway. The cost of peace in the short term rarely really matters. This particular misjudgment seems relatively minor when set beside Charest's achievements. As a former deputy prime minister and minister for the environment (he had headed the Canadian delegation at the Environmental Summit in Rio in 1992), Charest did not view, and did not need to view, internal party structure issues as central. Add to that his outstanding performance in the 1995 Quebec referendum and the fresh life he breathed into the Conservative Party, with a tenfold improvement in the 1997 election from two to twenty seats. And he did not make the misjudgment alone.

The key elements of a greater grassroots accountability were, first, a constitutional change to replace a broadly elected national executive with a national council made up of all riding association presidents, who could number as many as three hundred. The executive committee—made up of the broadly elected president and a few table officers, chosen without the approval of the national council—was able to act only in an interim way, and the council was itself unwieldy. The far more devastating aspect of this new regime was the replacement of the delegated leadership convention (for which party members gather in their riding associations to elect delegates who will then go to a convention to choose a leader) with a one-member, one-vote system, in which the members of riding associations voted directly for their leadership preference. Each riding, regardless of population or membership size, would get the same one hundred points on the leadership tally board. The supposed impact of this innovation was to enfranchise all party members, do away with the clout of the party establishment (MPs, senators, federal candidates, privy councillors, provincial MLAs, and so on), and do away with a brokered convention. It was meant to take leadership and accountability out of the back rooms.

The theory was compelling. Most of the party establishment saw it as a way to open up the political process to the rank and file. I saw it as an incentive for building new membership and one more reflective of younger Canadians who might otherwise feel squeezed out by an established and entrenched elite. In the end, however, we were all quite wrong. The change proved devastating to party fortunes, and it had consequences well beyond its actual impact on the leadership selection process.

First, the process was taken out of the back rooms, all right: it was thrown into the sub-basement, never to be noticed again.

Second, the evaporation of a significant leadership convention with any uncertainty or excitement meant that the party lost a critical opportunity to showcase new talent and ideas. TV networks will not cover anything that is not newsworthy. A fifth-place struggling political party could not afford to give up this kind of exposure. The 1998 leadership race was barely noticed outside the Conservative Party. In 2000, I remember sitting at a dinner at Queen's University celebrating the annual Gow Lecture, named after Donald Gow, an early director of the School of Policy Administration (now the School of Policy Studies). Premier Gary Doer of Manitoba was the lecturer. Donna and I were sitting with a former British high commissioner to Canada, who was visiting Queen's from London that year. I asked him about William Hague, the Tory leader in the UK, and what his chances were against Tony Blair in the coming election.

"Nil," was the peer's friendly response.

"Why don't you Tories try to put in a leader who can win?" I asked further.

"Well, as there is no chance—no one else really wants the job—sort of how, I assume, Joe Clark became leader in 1998."

My colleague Tom Courchene, who with Margie Courchene had joined us at table, looked up and said to the usually well-informed British diplomat, "Well, actually, Hughie and a few others had tried to beat Clark." Not only had no one noticed any of the names of 1998—such as who the other candidates were and what they stood for—but even the most astute Canada-watchers had no awareness that a leadership race had actually taken place.

Third, local riding associations depend on hard-working volunteers—volunteers who care as much about the Progressive Conservative cause as about any community charity or undertaking, and this move, by reducing their role as potential delegates, diluted their importance, standing, and presence in the community-based architecture of a national political party. This had the direct effect of weakening that local organizing and fundraising capacity precisely at the time in the party's history when the party's very survival needed it the most.

Fourth, at a traditional convention, delegates arrive either committed to a first-ballot choice or open-minded, then essentially come together on a final ballot. This is a process that starts with fragmentation and ends either with reconciliation or with the basis for reconciliation in the new leader's hands. However, in the new one-person, one-vote process, none of the main actors are in the same place at the same time on decision day. Furthermore, only riding totals and percentages—as opposed to votes and people—are recorded. This all makes reconciliation and the forging of a coherent unity after the choice much more difficult, something that is dangerous within the Conservative Party at any time—and that was possibly fatal at a time of rock-bottom national standing.

Besides, a political party is linked in its present and future to its past, both good and bad. And political parties have a hierarchy of those who have, largely as volunteers, served for decades. To dilute or diminish either the history or the historical connection is simply to weaken the brand and the lineage. This was the essence of what the great accountability proponents within the Conservative Party, as well as the Manning core, failed to understand. Without questioning the sincerity or public-spiritedness of either, they were, in essence, destroying a party tradition that Canadians knew and understood—one within which Canadians as diverse as Peter Lougheed, Lincoln Alexander, Flora MacDonald, Darcy McKeough, Jacques Flynn, Richard Hatfield, Diane Cunningham, Mike Harris, Claude Wagner, E. Davey Fulton, Ellen Fairclough, Bob Stanfield, Benoît Bouchard, Barbara McDougall, Don Mazankowski, Georges Valade, John Harris, Brian Peckford, Mary Collins, and Doug Harkness could all cooperate in the national interest. That tradition's disappearance would cause Canadians to worry about the new conservative forces, and who they really were, and what they really believed in. One person, one vote simply degraded the currency and meaning and transparency of party membership.

Yet these were the changes put into place under Charest, changes that in some way would make the outcomes of the 1998 leadership and the "to merge or not to merge" issue somewhat unavoidable. Interestingly enough, the populist Reform Party under Manning was not as open or democratic as the Conservatives. But Reform had the patina and narrative of a grassroots movement, which Manning marketed expertly, all the while keeping very tight central control. Reform created an image of populist bottom-up accountability, and the Conservatives decided to make huge structural changes to appear no less open or accountable. To the extent that this rendered the Progressive Conservatives less nimble and effective, it was a remarkable tactical win by Manning and his competent and determined inner circle of Reformers.

Charest, however, was in his person and character a unique problem for Reform. He was young, thoughtful, and steeped in national politics, with a network that spanned the country. As a key participant in the House of Commons committee process during Meech Lake, he was very much the nemesis of Bloc Québécois leader Lucien Bouchard. Yet his bilingualism and strong historical association with the moderate nationalist tradition in Quebec made him a perfect bridge between English and French Canada—he counted Alberta's Ralph Klein as a friend and as a sympathetic colleague, both having served as environment ministers. Moreover, he was freed from the House of Commons, as the Conservatives had neither official party status nor a fixed place in question period. Elsie Wayne, the irrepressible MP for Saint John, New Brunswick, was sufficiently media-savvy and outspoken to get as much media as, if not more than, the party had any right to hope for in connection with Commons debates. And in the lead-up to the 1997 federal election, there was a quiet but steely resolve by many not to let the grand old party of Sir John A. disappear.

It is fair to say that the party received, in the national media, on Bay Street, and in local media, relatively warm coverage. The country had seen the face of the opposition alternatives—the Bloc in Quebec and the Reform in the west. Large parts of Canada—in Ontario, urban Quebec, and the Atlantic—were not pleased with those options. Those parts of the country that had voted strongly in protest were not as one-dimensional as the parliamentary seat totals in 1993 suggested. Thousands who had voted Conservative in the west and Ontario, and in Quebec and the Maritimes, simply saw their votes set aside by our winner-take-all first-past-the-post system.

To be fair, the same happened to Liberal voters in the west and to Reform voters in Ontario. But even the most intensely anti-Conservative conceded that, at two seats in the House, the Tory party was unjustly underrepresented. After all, the 15 per cent of the vote the Conservatives gleaned in 1993 should have generated more than thirty-five seats. This created a mood that was sympathetic to Conservatives in general, and to the gregarious, articulate Charest in particular.

In 1994 and 1995, Charest attended fundraisers and annual meetings, met with prospective candidates such as Peter MacKay in Nova Scotia, and kept the party afloat. Conservatives were glad to see him. In his intensity, decency, and engagement, they sensed the essence of a new beginning. In his intellect, outreach, and compassion, they sensed a brand of conservatism with more potential than the sterile, on occasion xenophobic, and hellfire-and-damnation feel of the Reform Party under Manning. I say "feel" here because that impression may not have been totally justified. Manning had a caucus that very much reflected the "face of Canada," with more visible-minority MPs than the Liberals elected in 1993, or even than in the prior Conservative administration. And, as the more "national" burden of the Reform's parliamentary presence became apparent, some of the party's core narrative began to moderate on issues such as lax immigration rules, too liberal a use of the Charter of Rights and Freedoms by the courts (as if the judges had the choice of ignoring the Constitution), and "too much for Quebec."

Charest's repositioning of the federal party, the Chrétien father-knows-best bias of a disengaged federal-provincial dialogue, the Reform Party under Mr. Manning seeking to moderate its standing and appearance, and the Bloc Québécois led by a Lucien Bouchard at the top of his game as leader of the opposition in Ottawa—all these factors conspired to create volatile conditions for the 1995 Quebec referendum.

This referendum, set for October 30, 1995, would be, in a sense, the Waterloo for the Chrétien government's policy of wishing the unity issues away by simply not discussing them. When the referendum campaign began, the federal government urged other provincial governments to stay out, even though it had no discernible strategy of its own. Quebec was still in the throes of recessionary pressures, and the percentage of poor had increased markedly. Federalist triumphalism that saw one business leader speak early in the campaign of "crushing" the sovereigntists (the French verb used was *écraser*) ignited Quebeckers' sense of fair play against the federalist campaign. Chrétien had won his modest majority in 1993 without a meaningful number of French-language votes in Quebec outside Montreal. The Conservative Quebec infrastructure was, post-Mulroney, in serious if not potentially terminal disarray. Daniel Johnson, the decent, pragmatic, and courageous PLQ leader in Quebec and leader of the *non* federalist forces in the province, was undercut by Chrétien any time Johnson tried to build bridges between moderately nationalist federalist voters and the *non* side.

In the early weeks of the campaign, Ottawa's rigidity, when contrasted with the Quebec-affirming positive campaign of the *oui* side, laid the groundwork for disaster. Ottawa relied on polls that showed little movement in voter intentions. In essence, they were ignoring the old Allan Gregg rule about voter intention. As Gregg puts it, the four-inch ice pack does not start to crack *ab initio*—the water current underneath must first pick up wave velocity and punch, then the cracks begin from the bottom up. By the time they are seen on top of the ice, it is often too late for the change to be stopped. In the miasma of federal disarray, the forming cracks were being ignored. Ottawa's undercutting of Daniel Johnson, together with the PQ's wise decision to appoint Lucien Bouchard their designated chief negotiator for any post-referendum negotiations with Ottawa, made Charest the only consistently appealing and coherent pro-federalist force. The emotion, dedication, and energy Charest brought to the Canada side, his own position as underdog, his youth, and his facility made him the only compellingly sympathetic choice for the *non* side. And he campaigned like a banshee. Liberals, such as then finance minister Martin, either overstated their position or rang less than true. Martin's allegation that close to one million jobs would be at risk if Quebec chose sovereignty was discredited even as the speech was being distributed. What more did *oui* voters and potential *oui* voters need to feel relatively risk-free in their vote when one of the most competent federal ministers could not get it right and when the federal leader of the opposition, the respected Lucien Bouchard, would be Quebec's key negotiator?

Moreover, the PQ government was absolutely expert at ensuring that all aspects of "civil society," or "*les communautés culturelles,*" in Quebec received financial support from one citizenship or community program or another. Millions had been poured into even amateur hockey leagues, *âge d'or* seniors' groups, cultural organizations, and youth initiatives. Many Quebec ministries had assistant deputy ministers in the regions who helped ensure that no stone was left unturned. For many, this financial link with Quebec City, and the Capitale-Nationale, was a clear sponsorship link (in the purest sense of that word) between a future nation of

Quebec and their organizations' continued support. By and large, these local non-profit community groups were doing good solid work, and they were worthy of Quebec government support. But it was not support disengaged from the larger PQ goal of a sovereign Quebec. Ottawa's support of a volunteerism infrastructure in Quebec pre-1995 was not meaningfully competitive or as well rooted. The absence of Liberal federal MPs in Quebec in any great numbers outside of Montreal since 1993 made the imbalance even worse. The BQ members did excellent work in support of the PQ community-development mission.

The large final rally in the streets of Montreal at which Charest would speak—and to which thousands came from all over Canada (my wife and I took the day off from work to take the train in with many others from Sir John A.'s old riding of Kingston)—may not have changed the minds of many undecided voters, but to the extent that it solidified the *non* vote and intensified the sense of crisis, it did help. Post-referendum polls that implied that the rally was unhelpful were of the kind often done by pollsters who measure everything but value nothing terribly well. Charest's speech reflected his passion and engagement to both Quebec and Canada and his determination that neither need ever be exclusive of the other. It was Charest at his best, and it solidified the momentum necessary to narrowly deny the *oui* side a victory.

The 54,288-vote margin was small (1.16 per cent), but it probably represented the high point for the sovereigntist aspirations of a generation. It also destroyed complacency in Ottawa, which had begun to fray as referendum day came closer. Prime Minister Chrétien's angst and engagement near the end was too little, too late, but it at least portended activism to come.

A few weeks before referendum night, I had been drafted by Premier Harris to be a dollar-a-year constitutional adviser in the lead-up to the vote and for about two years thereafter. I knew both the deputy of inter-governmental affairs, Richard Dicerni, and the premier's chief, David Lindsay, from previous lives, and trusted them both. Dicerni had been a federal-provincial relations veteran of the federal public service and then in the Secretary of State and PCO before being lured away to Queen's Park by headhunters acting for the Rae government in 1992. Lindsay had been a stalwart in the provincial Tory research office for many years and had a solid reputation as a fair, bright, and reasonable policy adviser. Others involved with the premier as advisers, such as Leslie Noble, Paul Rhodes, and Ron McLaughlin (who had been on the student government executive with me decades earlier at the University of Ottawa), had worked with me in supporting Larry Grossman for leader back in 1984. The premier had gone to the Montreal demonstration with his son and had simply been one more Canadian in the crowd affirming his belief in Canada. But like other premiers, he had, along with his staff and ministers, been largely kept in the dark by Ottawa. Ottawa seemed very much to be an observer in the near demise of the country. I was stunned to find out that Ottawa and Ontario had barely had a conversation on a worst-case scenario.

By referendum night, finance deputies across the system had agreed to chat the next day. As we worked on draft statements and connected with various parts of the provincial system—treasury, intergovernmen-tal affairs, some overseas offices, parts of Ottawa—it was clear not only that the provinces had been excluded from the debate in Quebec, but that Ottawa's strategy was bluster and death-bed repentance rather than substantive engagement. What was particularly maddening was the obvi-ous precedent that should have been followed. In the 1980 referendum, Lougheed, Davis, Hatfield, and others had been actively engaged with Quebec, with constructive messages.

But it had been Chrétien's referendum to lose, with the *non* side beginning with a massive lead in the polls. As Parizeau self-destructed on referendum night, with his infamous reference to "money and the ethnic vote," it ended up being the referendum that Bouchard and Charest won— Bouchard for his cause, his career, and his reputation, and Charest for Canada and for his own personal standing as a Canadian and Quebecker absolutely passionate about the interdependence of both.

All of this would admirably prepare the Conservative leader for the federal election campaign two years later in 1997. In a sense, it set him up in terms of his persona and standing far better than the organizational activities of a national political party could ever do. As mentioned earlier, the obsession with party democratization meant that the time a national leader and party structure could have spent on campaign preparation was taken up instead with restructuring and with recalibrating the party's constitution on issues of accountability. The process was seriously time-consuming. A constitution review and consultation process had been established. Meetings were held across the country. A national party committee worked away at it for more than nine months between 1994 and 1996.

A simple look at the chronology of key party events during the Charest leadership underscores this point. In spring 1994, a comprehensive constitutional review was begun by Charest and the party. A constitution committee with representatives from all ten provinces and the two territories was established. Its mission was to consult broadly with the party membership on constitutional change over a six- to nine-month period. A year later, a new national executive (now called the management committee) was established, and provincial directors were elected, pursuant to the new constitution.

The new constitution, which was adopted in April 1995, made some critical changes beyond one person, one vote for any leadership process. First, the eligibility for membership in the Progressive Conservative Youth Federation was changed, excluding young people between the ages of twenty-five and thirty, making it a younger organization. Second, a national membership program, the first centralized membership list for any federal or provincial party in Canada (normally membership was established solely by local riding associations), was established, along with clear constitutional authority to certify local riding associations' legitimacy in terms of valid local riding constitution, real membership, bank filings, and the rest. This was a broad and serious shift to central control. The twice-annual meetings of the national council (including all riding presidents) became the new vehicle for "accountability" and "openness"—the supreme soviet of the Progressive Conservative Party. The council was (and this was a reason for the able Don McDougall of London to voluntarily step aside from the PC Canada Fund) made responsible for party finances, with the PC Canada Fund and party headquarters made answerable to it for financial activities. Usually the PC Canada Fund operated in a closed loop with the leader and a dotted line to the elected treasurer of the party. This change was clearly a response to the $10 million deficit inherited from the 1993 Campbell election. Perhaps most importantly, the leader lost the right to appoint the chair of the PC Canada Fund, the national director, and various other key roles. The leader could now only "recommend" those individuals to the party's management committee.

If one's eyes glaze over at this internal obsessiveness at a time when the party had but two seats and was technically bankrupt, it is because the internal vagaries of a party's constitution are often profoundly boring. Canadians had voted in part against the Progressive Conservative government, which was headed by Prime Minister Campbell, and in part against an incompetent campaign devoid of any message of hope or continuity or change, and in part against a tough recession. The party had chosen Campbell in open convention—hotly contested and for all to see. To the extent that there was an elite, it split between Charest and Campbell at that convention.

It is a credit to Charest that he made progress in the 1997 campaign despite the party's obsession with internal processes. The interesting question is how much better he and the Progressive Conservatives might have done if the platform, campaign, and organization planning had been more intense, multi-layered, and durable.

In the end, much of the result of the 1997 campaign, to the extent it was a distinct improvement, emerged from Charest's passionate debate performance and decent persona. His campaign had been logistically adequate and well managed, which, considering the limited resources of the party, is a tribute to Jodi White, Charest's closest political confidant and one of the brightest and most able people ever to work in Ottawa. A former chief of staff to External Affairs Minister Joe Clark, White played a critical role in Charest's leadership bid, which had come very close to eclipsing Campbell's bid at the convention in June 1993. She then served as the new prime minister's chief of staff and was a sane and steady hand during exceedingly difficult times. White took over the Charest campaign just days before the Liberals called the election in 1997, when others who had chaired the pre-campaign process were set aside by the leader. In difficult circumstances, she acted as campaign chair. Aided by the PC national secretary (an elected post), Dr. Kellie Leitch, she turned what could have been a policy and organizational disaster into a remarkable step forward for the party. Some Harris Tories, such as Leslie Noble,

Scott Munnoch, and Stuart Braddock, also stepped up to help and stayed through the campaign. White's work was in no small measure aided by Charest's almost flawless performance.

Why do I say "almost" flawless about Charest's performance? Because of two critical areas where the leader's lack of clarity cost the party key momentum.

Before the election was called in 1997, and subsequent to the National Policy Convention in Winnipeg in the summer of 1996, there was a tension within the party—and especially within the Ontario federal and provincial wing (Premier Harris having, in 1995, been elected in a major upset against the Lyn McLeod Liberals, who were far ahead in the polls, at the end of the Bob Rae government). The tension was over what the relationship should be between the Ontario campaign organization and policy thrust and those of the federal party. Successful Ontario Tory strategists such as Leslie Noble, Tom Long, and Alistair Campbell were eager to be helpful. They believed that the only way to advance a Conservative campaign was to have a conservative platform, which, on the face of it, seemed a wholly sound and constructive point of departure. This was no radical right-wing proposition: it merely suggested that the Conservatives should be the party of lower taxes, a restrained role for government, more respect for provincial autonomy under the Constitution, more choice for grain farmers relative to the Wheat Board, a stronger national defence, a redefined role for fisheries, and a closer relationship with our American allies.

However, because of the fixation on internal party restructuring and the drain of the referendum, work did not really begin on the platform till the last minute. This dynamic was further enhanced by the reality that, in most provinces, provincial Conservative parties and governments benefited from effective cooperation among provincial Tories, despite their divided loyalties at the federal level. Manning had decided some years earlier that the Reform Party would not contest provincial elections, which made provincial Conservatives and federal Reform supporters allies in provincial campaigns. This would be particularly true among provincial Tories in Ontario, Manitoba, BC, and Saskatchewan. In none of these provinces would provincial Tory leaders have any incentive to create tension with Manning and Reform. In other parts of the country, Reform was less of a factor, and federal and provincial PC supporters were essentially more centrist and quite hostile to Reform and Manning.

This framework was not so much about disunity as it was about the different tempos and exigencies of provincial and federal politics in Canada. Unlike in the United States, there is no common presidential, state, and congressional election schedule. Many provincial governments are elected as counterweights to the federal government of the day.

All of this (plus the even more confounding reality that, in Ontario, many of the same people who had voted Liberal to give Jean Chrétien almost every seat in Ontario in 1993 had voted Conservative in 1995 to elect Premier Harris) created a difficult decision tree for Charest. Then there was the perception of many in the party that the Ontario Conservative version of the federal platform was not broadly based. This view was advanced by Charest's then-pollster Bruce Anderson, who always opted for a more centrist approach, and it all created a bit of a dog's-breakfast platform problem for the national PC leader. Few would claim it as their own. No broad party meeting had approved it. Charest himself had not internalized it in any way.

As a result, the party began the 1997 campaign with a policy platform with no firm footing in the campaign or in its leader's own sense of what the right balance should be.

But what is also true is that the integration between the Ontario provincial organization and the federal Tory group did not conspire to help propel a Tory national victory—this in contrast to the Davis-Stanfield coalition that just about won the 1972 federal election, to the Davis-Clark coalition of 1979, and to the Davis-Mulroney coalition of 1984. While many Tory cabinet ministers did campaign for their federal PC cousins, Harris now sent a serious signal: without a clear, well-rooted team in Ontario and strong support from the premier and the provincial caucus, Charest could not make major progress—normally a vital harbinger of progress in Quebec and elsewhere.

That the Tories did not play a devastating price for this fogginess speaks to Charest's outstanding campaign skills. Still, the lack of coherence cost the party serious opportunities in Ontario and reduced a remarkable campaign that might have sharply shifted the political balance to one that made real progress but still left the party with a long way to go to re-enter the universe of real contenders. That would have to wait for another day and, it turned out, for another leader.

The other major flaw—a lack of clarity that sapped meaningful Conservative momentum near the crucial end of the campaign—was the issue of what might constitute an acceptable margin in a future Quebec referendum on separation.

Various voices in the country, including such Trudeau Liberals as Tom Axworthy, Reformers Manning and Stephen Harper, and some on Bay Street, had advanced the notion that breaking up a country on the basis of 50 per cent plus 1 of those who voted in a referendum in Quebec on a "woolly question" was simply unacceptable. Manning and Harper took the view that all Canadians had the right to be consulted. Prime Minister Chrétien, aided by his federal-provincial relations minister, the austere, doctrinaire, and intellectually acute Stéphane Dion, also argued clearly and precisely that 50 per cent plus 1 was not enough. This position was put into play by Chrétien at a point in the 1997 campaign when a reasonable balance on federal-provincial relations espoused by Charest was generating significant momentum in the polls in Quebec. What had caught Chrétien's attention was that Charest was gaining the moderate nationalist, soft federalist vote in Quebec at the expense of the Bloc Québécois and the federal Liberals. Chrétien did little to moderate his persona in Quebec as the leading proponent of a dominating federal government and of an excessive, almost simple-minded rigidity, with his death-bed repentance in the dying days of that nearly lost referendum, his legal reference challenge before the Canadian Supreme Court of Quebec's right to unilaterally separate, his rush to Parliament with resolutions affirming special status for Quebec (which he and Trudeau had fought against all their lives, especially when helping destroy the historic Meech Lake and Charlottetown accords). The Bloc was suffering from post-referendum and voter fatigue with the endless *question nationale*. Charest was a new voice, a fresh, fluently bilingual, and disarmingly pragmatic voice, made all the more clear by his impressive performance in both the English and French television debates. Early gaffes by BQ leader Gilles Duceppe (Duceppe wore a hairnet into a cheese factory—no doubt an appropriate public health practice, but something no party leader should do, which may just mean that food-processing plants should be banned from lists of campaign stops) also created some running room for Charest in Quebec.

Manning had made his partisan career-ending mistake of a campaign ad that arrayed a series of French-Canadian leaders (Chrétien, Charest, Duceppe, Bouchard, and others) and clearly implies (however the

Manning camp protested otherwise) that French Canadian leaders had had too great a say in our national politics.

Asking whether 50 per cent plus 1 was enough to declare independence was a way for all the established forces to put an end to Charest's momentum. When asked for his answer to the question, he failed to respond for three very long days. That hiatus saw the air come out of the Tory balloon in Quebec, a balloon that was also beginning to drive some voter intention in Ontario. What might have been a more than forty-seat national result ended up hobbled by winning only five seats in Quebec, with André Bachand from Asbestos being the most prominent. The old polarities had re-emerged, with the Reform Party in the west and the Liberals and Bloc in Quebec largely intact. This made the Reform Party the official opposition, replacing the Bloc and re-electing a bare but still viable Liberal majority. Manning had made no progress east of the Manitoba border. Except for Manitoba's Brandon-Souris riding, neither had the Tories made any progress to speak of west of Ontario. Where the Tories had added to their 1993 two-seat national total under Charest's 1997 campaign leadership was with four more seats in Quebec beyond Charest's own, most of which clustered around Charest's Sherbrooke riding, with a ray of light in Lac-Saint-Jean and serious breakthroughs in Atlantic Canada. The new PC total in the latter region was helped by provincial Liberal governments being in some disarray; by an unpopular series of unemployment insurance changes in the region introduced by New Brunswick's Liberal minister Doug Young, who lost his own seat; and by the strong campaign in the region by Alexa McDonough, the new NDP leader who won her own seat in Halifax, elected other New Democrats in the region, and split the Liberal vote in many Atlantic ridings. Strong Conservative candidates such as Bill Casey and Peter

MacKay in Nova Scotia helped immensely—the Liberals were wiped out in that province.

The Chrétien Liberals won, but with a clear sense that their unchallenged mastery of a fragmented parliament could not go on forever. Their new majority was barely five seats.

While the Great Leap Forward was not to be, the Conservative Party had been saved from the precipice, the Liberals had been regionally humbled, and Jean Charest had emerged as a major national though not yet a contending political force.

The critical linkage between provincial and federal Conservative parties had not been strengthened, but Manning's remarkable progress over the nine years from 1988 to 1997 had been blunted once and for all. If anything, the Ontario-federal Tory linkage was weakened, though there is room for reproach on either side. It was really only Diefenbaker in 1958 and Davis-Mulroney in 1984 who got that relationship right, to maximum electoral effect. Davis-Stanfield had come close in 1972 but could not sustain it in 1974. At other times it was a relationship hard to sustain. Despite the Charest-Klein friendship, 1997 saw no Tory progress in Alberta, and almost none anywhere else in the west. Getting the federal provincial parties together in every province, but especially in Ontario, remains to this day the key to any national aspirations the Conservative Party may embrace.

On election night 1997, however disappointed he may have felt, Jean Charest danced with his wife, Michèle Dionne, who herself had been a prodigious and persuasive campaigner, well liked and even loved in many parts of the country. Charest had every reason to be celebrated. This remarkable young man had been the critical force that sustained the federalist cause not two years earlier in Quebec's fingernail referendum.

Now, on this night, he had saved the Conservative Party from oblivion, making it if not yet a contender, at least a party that was once again an official part of Canada's Parliament, with twenty seats, a research budget, a new, young and dynamic caucus, and very compelling prospects. For many this would be accomplishment enough—but there was a sense in the country that night that for Charest, and, perhaps for the Conservatives, this was just the beginning.

8

The Clark Denial

Joe Clark's election once again to the leadership of the Progressive Conservative Party, in November 1998, was not the product of any long strategic plan on his part to recapture the Tory leadership that he had lost to Mulroney in 1983, some fifteen years earlier. He had been a stalwart member of all of Mulroney's cabinets. He had been treated very well by the prime minister, and the public and media perception of him was that he had served the PM with distinction and loyalty. In fact, had Charest either won in 1993 (when Clark and many others wary of Campbell had supported him) or stayed on to fight the 2000 federal election, Clark's 1993 retirement probably would have been final.

Charest's 1998 departure for Quebec provincial politics had opened the Conservative leadership prematurely. There really were no successors in the federal caucus. The party's prospects, while enriched politically by Charest in the 1997 election, were financially troubled and politically conflicted. Some in the west and in Ontario saw Charest as the only hope; others saw him as the major block to an amalgamation of the two parties on the right. The Alliance, established in 1996 out of the Reform Party, was continuing its pressure on the Tory base in non-urban Ontario, having ended second to the Liberals in more Ontario federal seats than did the Conservatives in 1997. In that campaign, Charest had elected one Conservative in Ontario—Jim Jones of Markham—in large measure because the Liberal nominee and the incumbent MP were wrapped up in an alleged résumé misrepresentation and divisive internal fight.

When Charest was called to lead the Liberals in Quebec, encouraged no doubt by financial forces that promised all the necessary liquidity for the Quebec battle and an end to liquidity for any ongoing federal Tory presence, the federal Conservatives were bereft of many compelling choices for leader.

When I entered the lists, I did so in the belief that the party needed a strong policy framework to build for the next election and to construct bridges to other conservatives and to Liberal switch voters. Clark's subsequent decision to campaign for leader was a surprise to many.

Having been a candidate, there is very little I can say about the 1998 race that would not seem self-serving. Clark won on the second ballot by a solid margin, having waged a relatively effortless, policy-free campaign. The vast majority of Conservatives seemed delighted and relieved. Although the lack of a convention ensured that few Canadians outside the reduced ranks of the Conservative Party had any idea that there was a race going on—not to mention who any of the participants were—the national press, the other opposition parties, the caucus, and the Liberal government were all pleased to have an individual of Clark's stature and reputation back in the saddle. While Charest had stayed carefully neutral, Mulroney and most of his ministers had supported Clark, as had premiers Klein and Filmon.

This was not a time for Conservatives to experiment. As most saw it, Clark was selflessly offering himself to protect the party's future. The support he received reflected the wide regard with which he was justifiably held in so many quarters, fuelled partly by the feeling of many, especially older members of the party, that he had not been well treated when he was deposed from the leadership in 1983.

Clark's return and the party's turn to him, however, were in some respects a collective act of denial that, while well intentioned, added some years to the period of conservative irrelevance and disconnect from the core politics and democratic competitiveness Canada desperately needed.

Consider, for example, that the strength of the David Orchard campaign indicated how the combination of reduced and struggling riding associations with the new one-person, one-vote non-delegate rule had weakened the party. The party had become in far too many ridings little more than a shell, easily penetrated and overrun. The Charest-era national membership innovation had not strengthened local ridings; in fact, it may well have unwittingly contributed to making them weaker— along with the end of locally elected delegates in any leadership process, diluting the community role of riding associations and their ability to attract first-rate volunteers and highly skilled candidates.

Furthermore, there was no pressing need for Tory policy, with Finance Minister Martin providing apparently conservative fiscal policy while fighting or reducing the deficit and with Manning (and later his successor as leader, Stockwell Day), offering policy to the right of Martin. There was certainly no need that the Tories could articulate. The failure of the party to embrace any clear policy direction or noteworthy platform in the 1997 campaign only deepened the policy deficit for the entire country.

While Irving Gerstein continued to manage the party's debt/deficit issue with immense agility, and while the banks were being more than fair, Peter Whyte—Charest's chair of the PC Canada Fund—was not able to make much overall progress; any normative balance-sheet assessment of the party's finances reeked of insolvency.

The party had failed to build a solid cooperative and working relationship with Mike Harris, the Ontario PC premier, who did have a solid working relationship with Manning. The choice of Clark, whatever other benefits may have ensued from it, would only worsen prospects on this front. Clark had never built a working relationship with Ontario provincial Conservatives, a key contributing factor to his 1980 defeat as prime minister and to his 1983 overthrow as leader. As well, the party's relationship with Alberta's Ralph Klein was notoriously cool. (Alberta Conservative premiers rarely if ever can be counted on to support Conservative prime-ministerial aspirants from their own province. I assume that a local turf war of some kind obtains.)

The Quebec Tory caucus elected with (and largely because of) Charest would be hard to sustain in the absence of Charest himself, who, in departing to lead federalist forces in Quebec, had become leader of the Parti Libéral du Québec.

And while Premier Bouchard would win the next Quebec election in 1998, he would do so with fewer votes than Charest, who came second. Bouchard was sustained by the first-past-the-post system and by the relative efficiency of the PQ vote in *le Québec profond*. Charest, however, had at least won a large opposition caucus and a plurality of votes—an auspicious start for a newly minted provincial party leader against a broadly popular and moderate premier.

In the 1997 election, Charest had increased the party's popular vote to just under 20 per cent, and its seat count to twenty. His own federal seat was lost to the Bloc Québécois in the subsequent by-election.

The challenges Clark faced as the "new" Conservative leader were intense. For most Canadians his return seemed natural, almost expected. For his own part, because of his standing as a former prime minister and foreign minister, he quickly and effectively assumed a media presence and profile that were disproportionate to the party's size. In fact, by November 1999, the Conservatives had surged to 24 per cent in the polls, with Reform essentially in single digits in the most populous parts of the country. The Canadian public was beginning, in 1998–99, to place a small candle in the window for Clark if for no other reason than familiarity, respect, and old times' sake.

Clark and I met in Toronto a week after the Tory leadership final ballot and just before a Tory fundraising dinner that Donna and I were attending to encourage loyalty to the new leader and to show the flag to Toronto-area Tories (I had outpolled Clark in most Toronto ridings). It was a warm crowd, and Clark did well. What was not known when the other leadership candidates and I rose when called, to polite applause, was the substance of my discussion with Clark not two hours earlier in his suite at the Royal York Hotel. It had been a friendly discussion. Clark had been gracious in responding positively to my request that those who had worked their hearts out for me in caucus—Peter MacKay from Nova Scotia, André Bachand from Quebec, Charlie Power and Bill Matthews from Newfoundland—not be penalized in the caucus and House structure of the parliamentary party. I especially made the case for the many policy-focused young Conservatives who had campaigned hard and had earned a role in the coming infrastructure. There was no pettiness or churlishness in any of Clark's response. Near the end of the discussion, I looked at him and mentioned that when one comes second on the first ballot and drops out on the second (I had urged my supporters to support Clark, not Orchard), one had two choices: stay around in the party and help, perhaps seeking a seat and playing a constructive role, or quietly get out of the way so that the duly elected leader would have a clear and uncluttered path. I asked him what his preference was. The reason the question needed to be asked was simple: the party could brook no further division. Clark had won the leadership fair and square. And, with a large personal campaign debt, I had to get busy with the rest of my life, in either a partisan or a non-partisan role. Clark's lack of enthusiasm for any continuing partisan role on my part made it clear that it was time for me to go. I resolved to give him the clear reign he clearly wanted. The honourable next career step would have to be non-partisan. But Clark did apparently send other messages, perhaps unwittingly, to other, more meaningful players.

In August 1999, a long-time Newfoundland Conservative MP left the Tory caucus to join the Liberals, citing the need to serve his riding's interests and needs. I had come to know Bill Matthews in the 1998 leadership campaign because he and Charlie Power had been two brave Newfoundland MPs who stood with me in my leadership bid, along with former Newfoundland attorney general and party leader Lynn Verge, against the Clark-Crosbie tide in Newfoundland and Labrador. Matthews's move to the Liberals and Power's departure in 2000 did not have to do so much with animus toward Clark as with a sense that the Conservative Party's purpose under Clark had become about its own survival—or

Clark's—and was no longer about serving Canada's or the region's public-policy needs.

It is difficult enough to get outstanding Canadians to set aside careers and family to serve as candidates in parties that appear able to form a government some day; it is even more difficult to attract people to do so when a party seems unable to do much more than simply survive. While the arrival of Angela Vautour in late 1999 from the New Brunswick NDP caucus was encouraging, it may have had more to do with the dynamics of Premier Bernard Lord and his newly minted Tory provincial government. And, for reasons that may have gone back to a university rivalry between Clark and Manning—not to mention Manning's candidacy against Clark in the 1988 federal election in High River—Clark seemed determined not to pursue efforts to unite the right, but instead to sustain fragmentation in almost every way imaginable.

In September 1999, at the annual and general meeting of the PC Party in Toronto, held in the Constellation Hotel near the airport, Clark forces pushed for and received quasi-unanimous support for the 301 Resolution. This resolution called for the party to run a candidate in every federal riding, even when doing so would ensure a Liberal victory in that seat. The Clark initiative essentially put paid to the notion that unity on the right might be built by an approach that saw Alliance-Reform members in the west and Conservatives in the east and in the centre maximize their gains against the Liberals so that Liberal hegemony did not become a perpetual reality. It would also allow the two brands of conservatism to coexist, as opposed to pillorying each other. Whatever the merits of this approach—and the approach was not without weakness—it seemed to have more prospects than did internecine war between the factions of the right. Yet it was killed dead in September 1999.

Clark's motivation is understandable: any sign of weakness would have weakened his options as leader, and his party's options even more.

The problems faced by a national party that has had candidates in every riding for decades and that then decides not to do so completely should not be underestimated. Liberals in the east and in Quebec would have said "a vote for Clark is a vote for Reform." And in the west, there could be a few gains for Reform-Alliance candidates, who already held a majority of seats in every province west of Thunder Bay. For Conservatives to desert a series of ridings where, in the west especially but also in some ridings in southwestern Ontario the battle with Reform had been truly tough, would signal to those riding associations that had fought the hardest to stay alive against the Reform onslaught that, well, in some way, for them the fight was over.

To be fair to Clark, there was more than just nostalgia in this concern. The additive proposition that one often heard advanced—that the 20 per cent of the voters represented by the Charest Tories plus the almost 20 per cent represented by the Manning Reformers would produce a 40 per cent plurality—was never interregionally or nationally true. In many parts of the west, the addition would simply be wasted, as Reform won ridings quite handily. It is important to note that in Ontario, where the addition was meant to work best, most PC voters picked the Liberals as their second choice. This was also true of many Reform voters who, having joined as anti-Quebec Mulroney-haters, preferred Liberals—especially Martin Liberals—to their local Progressive Conservatives. In fact, when the parties did finally come together for the 2004 election, the combined vote percentage of the new party did not equal the respective totals of the old parties. Where the case for the benefits could have been and needed to be made was in the need for a coherent alternative government in opposition, an alternative Canadians could turn to when the time for change came.

The allocated-riding strategy (in which all sitting Reform and PC candidates would be grandfathered and only one conservative candidate run in each) was a two-election strategy. In the first election, the two parties would elect a hundred or so MPs and then, with relatively strong parliamentary wings, they would begin to work more or less as equals and build a new national party. Clark utterly rejected this strategy.

But Clark's rejection of change or adaptation did not stop time. The Reform Party, with meaningful support from provincial Conservatives across Canada—such as Tony Clement in Ontario, Clayton Manness in Manitoba, and Ralph Klein in Alberta—met in January 2000 to found the Canadian Alliance, building on Manning's "Think Big" admonition of 1988. In that same month, Newfoundland Tory MP Charlie Power resigned his seat in the House. In April of that year, André Harvey, the Tory MP from Chicoutimi–Le Fjord, resigned the Tory caucus to sit as an independent.

While the forces of attrition were working against Clark, the forces of change were afoot in the new party. In July 2000, Stockwell Day, a new, telegenic, passably bilingual former finance minister from Alberta, was elected to the leadership of the Alliance. Articulate, young, and with a great sense of political flair, he had defeated Manning. He had also beaten Tom Long, the savvy, thoughtful small-c conservative candidate from Ontario, who had come a third on the first ballot. In the end, Day won in Ontario against both Manning and Long. Long had been one of Premier Harris's most influential advisers, someone who had joined the Harris cause when the Ontario Conservatives were in third place and without money or prospects. His organizational and campaign skills were, and still are, compelling. He joined colleagues such as Leslie Noble (a senior

Harris party official who had supported Grossman for Ontario PC leader in 1985), whose riding organizational linkages and logistical skills were legendary; Paul Rhodes, the ultimate communication guru; and John Laschinger, who had chaired Harris's successful leadership campaign to create the Common Sense Revolution in Ontario, with Harris as its able and focused leader. While Long did not win the leadership, his presence in the race sent a critical message to Ontario Conservatives: that the Alliance was not only the Manning Reform Party; that the federal conservative cause in Ontario was now best advanced through the Alliance— and that whatever Clark was up to, it was no longer politically relevant. Not everyone in the federal or provincial Conservative parties in Ontario bought Long's message, but it had been sent.

With Tony Clement assuming the presidency in the United Alternative (precursor to the Canadian Alliance), with the obvious blessing of Premier Mike Harris, another clear message was being sent. Clement had been the provincial party president who had, along with Peter Van Loan, stood with the provincial party after its crushing defeat in 1987, when it was bereft of money and staff. Clement, then a young lawyer, had assembled a broad provincial corps of volunteers, including Amanda Walton, Dr. Kellie Leitch, Karen Schnarr, Blair McCready, Peter Atkins, Hugh Mackenzie, and Alexander Grieve. They joined volunteers such as John Tory, Michael Daniher, Stella Cicollini, and others province-wide who were determined to keep the provincial party alive. They did so with thousands of hours of volunteer work. They ran HQ functions, organized riding associations, raised money, attracted new talent, wrote policy, organized conventions, and kept the flag of Drew, Kennedy, Frost, Robarts, and Davis very much flying in the politics of Ontario. These were people who had linkages and networks across the province—in Van Loan's case, across the nation. And because they were based in Ontario, Clark's old myopia about Ontario largely excluded them from his inner circle.

Whether they preferred Day or Manning was less important than their preference for Conservatives to stay united federally and provincially. Some no doubt would have wanted Harris to be prime minister and were lukewarm to Clark or Charest as a result. Some were proponents of Charest as prime minister and deeply resented the apparent atrophy of the federal party under Clark.

All of this was very much on the boil when Jim Jones, the party's only Ontario MP, left the Tory caucus to join the Canadian Alliance.

In a by-election on September 15, 2000, Stockwell Day was elected in the riding of Okanagan-Coquihalla and Clark was elected in the Nova Scotia riding of Kings-Hants, aided by the then-Tory incumbent MP, Scott Brison, who resigned his safe Tory seat so Clark could run. More importantly for Clark's future and the PC Party's prospects, the party's national president, Peter Van Loan, stepped down—because Clark essentially demanded it. Clark had been told, erroneously, that Van Loan was organizing against him within the party. In fact, Van Loan had been trying to deal with wide party discontent about the rudderless, policy-free, organization-light, no-cash tenure of the Clark leadership. In doing so, he had been touring and listening to discontent and trying to manage it for both the leader and the party—precisely the job a national president has always done. The previous May, at the national policy convention, rumours had been widespread about a Clark resignation—rumours strengthened by his failure, until then, to identify a seat to run for to gain entry to the House of Commons. Clark's inability to work with Ontario Conservatives in 1979–80 had contributed to his final defeat in the country in 1980 and within the party three years earlier; in like manner, his sidelining of Van Loan and all the young Conservatives who were building the Ontario party would presage the ultimate failure of his second term as national leader.

The successful step ahead of his by-election was in September. But even the victory of Loyola Hearn in Charlie Power's old St. John's West seat the following May could not prevent the further attrition of federal party under Clark. By summer 2000, some opinion polls had the PCs plummeting from 24 per cent to 6 per cent, with the Liberals and Alliance gaining at Clark's expense. In September of that year, two Quebec Tory MPs from the Eastern Townships—Diane St-Jacques and David Price—deserted the party to join the federal Liberal caucus. In October, André Harvey set aside his independent MP status to join the Liberals. When the enthusiastic but inexperienced Day called in the Commons for an election, Prime Minister Chrétien obliged the leader of the opposition gladly. In the November 27 election, Chrétien kept the new Liberal seats in Quebec, added back some that had been lost to Charest in 1997, and maintained a strategic hold on Ontario, forming an enhanced majority and beating the Bloc Québécois in both seats and popular vote in Quebec for the first time since the Bloc entered the fray.

The Conservatives under Clark won only twelve seats. Their 12 per cent of the popular vote was the worst in the history of Canadian elections, 3 or 4 points below what Campbell had been able to achieve in the slaughter of 1993.

The Alliance under Day broke through with three seats in Ontario, and more seats overall than under Manning. Clark's winning of his own seat in Calgary and the saving of party status by André Bachand's razor-edge victory in Quebec created the sense, at least in the national media, of a moral victory for him.

In the TV debate, Clark had performed superbly, and Day, badly served by campaign and staff, looked more like an opposition leader than a prospective prime minister. Yet Day had probably moved the Alliance farther than Manning ever could have done, and he reduced the Tory party from having had prospects, in 1997, to once again being on the verge of oblivion. The media sense of a Clark surge near the end sustained new if insubstantial relevance for Clark past the election. Day's party had appeared incapable of explaining his rational and respectable stance for new flexibility in health care delivery and more confederal respect for the roles of the provinces. Yet he had done better electorally in more Ontario ridings than Clark had, and in some ridings, Liberals had been elected because of Tory and Alliance splits. He outpolled the Clark Tories in Quebec.

Clark's campaign skills, his personality, and his debating performance had saved the party from an end that his own period of leadership had made almost unavoidable. The Conservatives in 2000 had 40 per cent fewer seats and 40 per cent fewer votes than they had achieved under Charest in 1997.

So the period of denying the reality of the young generation of new Conservatives eager to build bridges in Ontario, of denying the importance of policy and ideas for the Conservative Party, had borne its inevitable fruit: an increased Liberal majority; the eclipse of Conservative prospects and seats in Ontario, Quebec, and the west; and the dilution of any coherent Conservative presence in the policy debates and deliberations of Canada and Canadians.

The Progressive Conservative Party was just about done.

PART 2

Finding a New Way

9

The Alliance Insurgency

The Tory defections, the Tory collapse in the polls, and the huge election setback did not, of course, take place in a vacuum. Politics not only abhors a vacuum, the broader context always ensures that any vacuum is filled, and quickly. The re-election of Prime Minister Chrétien in the 2000 election, the increase in his majority, the continued role of the Bloc Québécois, the sense that the Parti Québécois now faced formidable opposition from both the Charest Liberals and Mario Dumont's Action Démocratique all conspired to spark the leadership question in both the Liberal and the Alliance parties. In the Liberal Party, the Martin crew were concerned that Prime Minister Chrétien would settle in, taking 2000 as an indicator because of the modestly weakened Bloc in Quebec—and that settling in would diminish the Martin opportunity. In the Alliance, there was serious restiveness over the management of the campaign and a sense that a major breakthrough opportunity had been squandered even though it was the best Reform/Alliance showing ever. The Manning faction were not yet satisfied to move into statesman land, and there were caucus leaders who had not fully reconciled to Day's leadership.

Inexplicably, the Alliance seemed to have begun to fracture on its own expectations—expectations that Stockwell Day would simply win an election first time out. Not only was the expectation remarkably unfair (and without significant historical precedent) but in the context of someone elected to the House of Commons for little more than a few days before the election call, it was also completely unreasonable. To be fair to rank-and-file Alliance members, it was an expectation encouraged by Day and his entourage. In a general sense, Day was made to wear the defeat (along with the sad cardboard sign prop displayed at the TV debate) quite personally. And while most party leaders are allowed at least two runs in a national campaign, it became clear that forces in the party associated with Manning and others, and key players in the national caucus, would not allow Day a second one.

In January 2001, the national caucus of the Conservatives, along with key figures from the provincial Conservative parties of Ontario, Manitoba, and Alberta, and some leading Alliance-Tory switch hitters, met in London, Ontario. In a long and engaging conference, there was a general agreement that some forms of cooperation with the Canadian Alliance were needed, but no agreement was reached on the kind and structure of that cooperation.

There was relief among Conservatives that their party had retained official party status and that Clark had won his seat. However, the core reality of the 40 per cent seat and popular vote losses and of the party's continued financial stress had sunk in among the Tory rank and file across the country. The west was still a disaster area, only the Alliance had broken through in Ontario, and the Liberals were back on the march in Quebec and in the Atlantic regions. The party not only lacked a secure base, it also had no meaningful prospects for growth.

The Alliance, on the other hand, had now campaigned in three elections—two under Manning and one under Day—in which any significant breakthrough beyond the Ontario-Manitoba border had proven utterly unattainable. Moreover, the media expectations garnered and dashed by the Stockwell Day phenomenon seemed to have lowered the party's national credibility even further. On the face of it, it seems patently absurd that Day should have been dismissed despite the increased seat count and popular vote and Clark celebrated after having lost both. However, that was the mood of the country and the temper in most of the media. A "congenial truth" (what William Fox in his book *Spinwars* defines as a popular conception of the truth, not necessarily true itself) was alive in the land—that Clark had emerged with stature enhanced and Day with prospects dashed.

In the summer of 2001, the Alliance caucus entered a period of deep turmoil, with a minority of MPs reaching out quietly to test the possibility of some joint parliamentary or other collaboration with the Tories. This, of course, fell on receptive ears, especially among party organizers and bagmen who knew it was impossible for the Tories to soldier on unreinforced. Clark's initial instincts were supportive, but, consistent with his approach on the 301 Resolution, the Tory leader focused on making sure his personal control was not diluted in any meaningful way.

Clark agreed to a conference. Fifty delegates from both the PC and Canadian Alliance parties met at Mont Tremblant in August 2001 to discuss parliamentary collaboration in general and democratic renewal in particular. This meeting was sanctioned by both leaderships and had broad if not unanimous support from both parties' rank and file. A framework of what might shape some terms of union was agreed to, but it was not an agreement awash in specifics.

Early in July, before the Mont Tremblant understanding was in place, a group of dissident Alliance MPs (Chuck Strahl, Deb Grey, Grant McNally, Inky Mark, Jay Hill, Val Meredith, and Jim Pankiw) announced their formal disaffection with the Alliance leader and their breakaway from the Alliance caucus. They formed the Democratic Representatives Caucus (DRC, or DR) and agreed to join with the Tories in the House to form the PC-DR Coalition. DR members were integrated into the shadow cabinet. Clark was overall leader of the party and coalition, Elsie Wayne remained the Conservative Party's deputy leader, and Chuck Strahl was deputy leader of the coalition.

This was a period of some optimism in Conservative circles. Strahl was warmly applauded at provincial and federal Tory fundraisers around the country, and he spoke well and often.

Within the Alliance, there appeared to be two schools of thought in reaction to the DRC. One group's hatred of Clark and the Tories precluded any tolerance for those seen as defectors to the Clark Tories. The other group was so negative about Day's leadership that they were mildly—and very quietly—supportive of the DRC group as a destabilizing tactic. Both groups had sizeable pluralities who ultimately saw the need for a combined conservative party. Among the members of both those groups and the DRC were supporters of Stephen Harper as leader to replace Day.

It was apparent within the Alliance and a large group of United Alternative Conservatives (namely federal Alliance and provincial

Conservative proponents of "one conservative party") that Harper possessed the policy depth, the economics training, and the professional background to be both the logical next step for the party and the most acceptable to many Conservatives. Harper had experience with the Progressive Conservatives (having worked with Jim Hawkes, a long-time Conservative MP) and the early Reform initiative (having been a policy chief at Reform HQ and executive assistant to the then newly elected Deborah Grey). Adding to his bona fides were his respectable capacity in French; his background on the intellectual side of the conservative debate in Canada; his friendship with such conservatives as David Frum, Tony Clement, and Linda Frum; and the civility of his relations even with conservatives of a less muscular ideology. To top it all off, he had been elected in 1993 from Calgary as a Reform MP, later stepping out of Parliament in 1997 to be close to his family.

But for his opportunity to come, the dynamics of the Alliance insurgency had to play out a bit.

The announcement on September 10, 2001, of the new PC-DRC coalition in the House was understandably overshadowed by the next day's terrorist attacks on the World Trade Center and the Pentagon.

With the government stepping up to the plate on security issues and its armed forces deployment to Afghanistan, leadership pressures within the Liberal Party and leadership and organizational pressures within the Canadian Alliance Party receded from the headlines and from the political radar screen.

And for reasons that may have seemed relevant at the time, after a brief focus on security and deployability matters, Clark began a multi-month, obsessive focus on the minutiae of the so-called Shawinigate scandal. The *National Post* had alleged in a series of articles that the prime minister of Canada had an undue connection to a loan made to the Grand-Mère hotel in his riding by the Business Development Bank of Canada, a Crown agency. The hotel's proximity to a golf course in which Chrétien had held an interest, some somewhat sloppily executed trust or share sale documents allegedly affecting the prime minister's alleged interest, and the relative timing of these were all meticulously addressed in the House by Clark, along with the details of a wrongful dismissal suit between the released CEO of the Business Development Bank and the bank's board. The amounts of money involved were not substantial, nor was there any allegation that Chrétien had profited in any way from his supposed perfidy. Nevertheless, Clark's ardour was second to none in the House. While his caucus joined him in asking questions about other public priorities, most of the press coverage of Clark and his party was about the so-called Shawinigate Affair—and this at a time when the large gaps in our defence capability had begun to reach apparent crisis proportions, when the reality of fiscal disequilibrium was clearly diluting provincial capacities in health, education, and social welfare, and when the government's incapacity relative to Canada-U.S. relations was leaping off the public page. If patriotism is the last refuge of scoundrels, then surely scandalmongering is to some the highest act of patriotism, especially for those with little else to offer. Because of media euphoria over scandals of even the most Lilliputian dimensions, politicians are easily sucked in. The problem in these cases, of course, is that while such scandals may not be salient enough to attract public interest or in any way affect voter intentions, they eat up great amounts of media, political, emotional, and managerial time and energy, tend to discredit the entire system, and, in the end, change very little indeed.

Coherent policy work on economic, social, and geopolitical frameworks might have broadened PC-DRC reach within the House and within the memberships of the two parties, but time for this was lost, and in politics, lost time and lost opportunities can never be regained.

The Alliance insurgency continued that fall with Day announcing his retirement from the leadership to be free to run in a new leadership convention and to contain and deal with the destabilizing elements of the party once and for all. Remarkably, he made this announcement at the Ritz Carlton Hotel, the grande dame of Sherbrooke Street in Montreal and the site of the famous profession of loyalty between Mulroney and Clark in 1983.

As 2002 began, the pressure for a Harper entry increased. Meanwhile, other candidates, such as Grant Hill and Diane Ablonczy, emerged to challenge Day and the Alliance appointed an interim leader.

The Conservatives ambled into the New Year with their momentum slowed, their opportunities slipping away, and their finances continuing to dwindle, although, to his credit, Irving Gerstein had succeeded in "restructuring" the party debt with the tactical use of a small trust fund (the Bracken Trust). This fund was put together when party headquarters at 178 Queen Street in Ottawa were sold to Metropolitan Life to make way for an office tower. The restructuring had the effect of reducing the total amount owed by the party, reducing the present value of the remaining debt and reducing net interest costs for the Progressive Conservatives. It gave the fiscally strapped party of John A. Macdonald breathing room, and not a moment too soon.

But relations between Clark and the DRC were strained at best, non-existent at worst. Clark's MO of being too aloof and self-focused to reach out had reasserted itself. Despite the efforts of the Democratic Representatives MPs (and the supportive efforts of Tory MPs in working together), any sense of a larger game plan to coalesce a national opposition and a real alternative government in order to render Canada's democracy once again competitive was utterly absent. The frustration of DRC members was palpable, as, to a lesser extent, it was on the Tory side of the House. Some Tory members felt Clark was spending too much time with the DRC members; some DRC members, meanwhile, could not quite understand the relative lack of regular contact with Clark. To some extent, this was unfair to Clark, who was trying to balance those of his rank and file who were opposed to full integration and others who were remarkably gung ho—not easily done under the best of circumstances.

By March 20, when Harper won the Alliance leadership handily over Day (and was very much the pro-choice candidate of the two), the sense of new Alliance momentum, on the one hand, and arrested Tory development, on the other, had well set in.

On that Friday, Chuck Strahl penned an open letter calling for the union of the two parties. By April 2, an emergency meeting of the coalition caucus was called in Calgary to address rumours that the dissidents who were part of the DRC would be returning to the Canadian Alliance. A new but tentative agreement was patched together but it was to be fleeting.

Not seven days later, on April 9, at its regular Wednesday caucus meeting, the PC-DRC coalition founders—except for Manitoba MP Inky Mark—returned to the Alliance under its new leader. In the war of attrition between the Alliance and the Tories, the Tories had wasted an opportunity presented by the Alliance insurgency and had squandered the time necessary to have a major impact on the policy agenda for Canada's centre-right parties. The Alliance had moved on from a leader, in Day, whose personality and telegenic skills had come to be viewed (probably quite unfairly) as of insufficient *gravitas* for leadership of a government to a bright, young, attractive, and thoughtful leader who showed early determination to broaden and consolidate the Alliance base.

This was a huge letdown for the rank and file of the Conservative Party and for its financial supporters, volunteers, and caucus members. There was no fallback strategy. In fact, the entire DRC "strategy" was really the Alliance dissidents reaching out and forcing a joint coalition strategy on the Clark Conservatives. Tory caucus MPs had put massive amounts of time into the effort, chairing joint policy meetings and holding back-to-back twinning meetings between riding associations in the Atlantic region, BC, and the Prairies. Now they felt deeply and personally cheated. Bay Street, the oil patch, and rue Saint-Jacques were all despondent that no party seemed likely to give the Liberals any challenge at all. Not even the victory of Charest over Bernard Landry in Quebec or the May by-election win in Gander–Grand Falls by PC Rex Barnes could raise the spirits of the rank and file.

That summer saw the rumblings of a caucus insurgency against Clark's leadership and a wide range of rumours from different sources of his intent to resign.

On August 6, indicating that he had taken the party as far as he could, Clark announced his resignation. It was just fifteen days before the PC Party annual and general meeting, which had been called for August 22–25 in Edmonton. At that meeting, potential leadership candidates such as John Tory, Bernard Lord, and Peter MacKay produced a great sense of excitement. David Orchard's dogged determination to turn the party into an agrarian, neo-Luddite, narrow nationalist party focused on anti-American excess resurfaced, and the riding-weakening rules for leadership selection, which still pertained, were open for him to exploit.

Inky Mark, the independent MP from Manitoba who had not gone back to the Alliance, chose the Edmonton meeting to formally join the Tory caucus, which, with Clark helpfully staying in his Calgary Centre riding and including Barnes of Newfoundland, brought the party's standing to fourteen.

Yet as 2002 came to an end, both the Alliance and the Conservatives were faced with the inevitability of a Martin prime ministership tied to a broad sense in the country that Martin had set Canada's fiscal house straight, was less rigid and more confederal than Chrétien, and was more at home within the broader international community, especially with the Americans. He was seen as more likely to get along with the new Charest government in Quebec and less confrontational overall. Chrétien was basically compelled to give way. He announced at a Liberal meeting in Quebec in August 2002 that he would be stepping down as leader at the end of 2003 and as prime minister as early as March 2004. His hand had been forced by the Martin Liberal Party forces outflanking him on the ground on delegate selection for general meetings and local riding fights in BC, the Atlantic, and large parts of the Prairies, Ontario, and Quebec—and especially among young Liberals. The timetable was a little depressing given just how long Chrétien and his office and supporters could control events within the party, but the transition, so long in the waiting, was now underway. While various Chrétien-friendly candidates such as Allan Rock and John Manley surveyed the turf, they would soon find that tireless, decade-long work of the Martin forces had made sure there was little if any turf to survey. Prominent and capable Liberals, such as Warren Kinsella for Rock and Herb Metcalf for Manley, would find that Mike Robinson, David Hurley, Dennis Dawson, and John Duffy had done remarkable work as volunteers and Martin supporters, never having let the flame go out after the Chrétien win over their man in Calgary in 1990. Hard work in the vineyard has its consequences, and for Martin they were all positive.

With the disarray of two competing conservative parties and no coherent choice for Canadians who might not want a Liberal government, easy and glib predictions of more than two hundred Liberal seats were heard from all quarters of the country. Two Conservative parties, one with a new dynamic and deeply strategic leader in Stephen Harper, and another in search of a leader, a bank account and a mission, seemed like easy pickings for a Liberal Party about to choose a popular finance minister, Paul Martin, to assume an easy Liberal majority—and further harden the "default" preference of Canadian voters.

10

The MacKay Bridge

With the resignation of Joe Clark in August 2002, the Conservative leadership derby began in earnest.

Various names entered the public domain, though more in idle speculation than as substantive options. John Tory; Larry Smith, then publisher of the Montreal *Gazette;* Sandy Riley, the successful CEO of Great-West Life in Winnipeg; Jim Dinning, the former treasurer of Alberta; Jim Flaherty, former Ontario treasurer—all were speculated on in various contexts. Even my own name was bandied about.

In the end, the candidates were Peter MacKay, the affable young Nova Scotia MP and House leader who had worked so hard with Chuck Strahl to try to make the PC-DRC coalition work; Jim Prentice, the PC Party treasurer and a long-time party volunteer in Alberta; Scott Brison, MP, the Clark-team loyalist who had campaigned ruthlessly for his man in 1998 and surrendered his seat for the leader's ultimate re-entry to the House; Craig Chandler, a new face—a man totally focused on uniting with the Alliance; André Bachand, the MP for Asbestos, who believed that Quebec should not be unrepresented in the race; David Orchard, whose strength in the party had grown as a direct result of the weakness of the party nationwide; and Heward Graffety, a Clark-era cabinet minister, one of the few Conservatives repeatedly elected in Quebec, and a man who, while viewed (unfairly) by some as eccentric, brought a strength of character and decency to the race for as long as he stayed in it.

But the polling numbers, both private and public, were very clear about the commanding position that MacKay had in the hearts of the rank and file. MacKay had not only soldiered on in the House, he had also been to almost every riding association, provincial annual meeting, and policy conference across the country. He campaigned for other nominated candidates and was there when riding associations or young Conservatives called. In the days of the PC-DRC coalition, he was also on the road to DRC riding associations to help blend the brands.

There was no riding association too small and no meeting too remote for MacKay to attend. He even had the raw courage to support me in the 1998 leadership in a province that was an absolute wasteland for our campaign, which meant he understood the nobility of the compelling but losing struggle. As a former Nova Scotia Crown attorney (let go by that province's Liberal government when he won the local federal Tory nomination pre-1997), he, like his father, former MP Elmer MacKay, was absolutely determined to hammer Liberals in the House at the first rumour of a scandal—even if there was substantially less to the scandal than met the eye. But that did get him media attention, and none of that hurt. Conservatives across the country saw him as the logical leader, and as the next generation of Tory leader. While Brison and Prentice worked hard and campaigned with eloquence and spirit, the core numbers kept MacKay in the lead for the duration of the campaign.

The leadership rules committee had approved a significant change in the process that would make the convention of May 31, 2003, far more significant than the non-convention of 1998. They had essentially borrowed the formula used by the Ontario provincial Liberals, in which the first vote of riding delegates was in fact determined by the votes in the ridings of all Conservative Party members, and the second ballot was in the hands of the delegates themselves. So this scheme, in a sense, had the best of both worlds—a more universal suffrage in the party and a public decision-making dynamic at the convention were built into the overall process. It was a substantial net improvement.

By the time the convention rolled around, MacKay and his opponents had criss-crossed the country. Graffety and Bachand had pulled out of the campaign. The main contenders were MacKay, Brison, Orchard, and Prentice. But Orchard had built meaningful strength and would outlast the Tory veterans and long-time Clark supporters beyond the first ballot, which MacKay easily topped. There was immense controversy in the party about what transpired next, a controversy that seems somewhat overblown in terms of the brokering that goes on at any leadership convention.

As the final ballot approached, the Brison people had gone to Prentice, a very attractive and gentlemanly political personality; Prentice had stood down from the riding in which he had been nominated when Harper ran there in a by-election to regain entry to the House after being chosen Alliance leader over Stockwell Day in March of 2002. Prentice had argued that promoting unity between the two parties would not be helped by running against Harper. Now there was a statistical possibility, if not the political reality, that Prentice could overcome MacKay on the final ballot, with Orchard's support. As Orchard was hostile to any cooperation with the Alliance—and of the meaningful candidates, Prentice was most in favour of that rapprochement—the likelihood that many "Orchardistas" would join the Prentice squad was not overwhelming. MacKay had been the clearest about not being "the party merger candidate." While always talking about "finding a common ground to unite Conservatives from coast to coast," he was far less prone to a priori ideological affinities with the old Reform crowd. He was very much a Maritime conservative, reflecting a strong Stanfield Tory mix of social justice and equality of opportunity, with more than a soupçon of support for law and order thrown in from his days as a Crown attorney.

Both the Prentice people and the MacKay people needed Orchard's support. In the end, it went to MacKay, who, despite being the logical choice for Orchard, signed a sketchy note to the latter about giving some Orchardistas a role in party headquarters, not merging with the Alliance/Reform party, and reviewing free trade.

Before and after MacKay's victory on the last ballot, when the Orchard folk leaked the note to the press, some in the rank and file were troubled. The vast majority of Progressive Conservative Party members saw Orchard and his people, rightly or wrongly, as non-Conservative, Maude Barlow–inspired anti-American New Democrats too extreme for even that party. Orchard himself liked to build his case on the Diefenbaker-era opposition to nuclear warheads on our Bomarc missiles and lack of Canadian preparedness to engage in the red-level alert during John F. Kennedy's confrontation with the Cubans and Soviets in 1962–63. His rather nostalgic view of Diefenbaker glossed over the collapse of the Tory government over the issue, over the stark divisions in the cabinet, and over the fact that U.S. ambassador Adlai Stevenson had actually displayed to the United Nations Security Council the photographs of Soviet missile installations some 150 kilometres from Florida. It also seemed to skip over the hard-fought seminal campaign of 1988, in which rank-and-file Progressive Conservatives across Canada battled long and hard for the free trade agreement negotiated between the two countries. Nevertheless, the weakened and steadily further weakening state of the PC Party under Clark, the party's obsession with internal governance and accountability at the expense of policy and outreach, had made the penetration and takeover of many local riding associations possible for Orchard and his supporters in Saskatchewan, British Columbia, and parts of Ontario—associations that the Orchardistas had, to their credit, worked hard and well.

The future of any political party is, in the end, in the hands of those who show up, and Orchard's supporters had shown up in large numbers at riding conventions and at larger regional policy meetings. So, however distasteful it may have been to many, the Orchard people had earned their influence at this meeting through their own hard work, which in an open, democratic party is supposed to count for something most of the time.

So the angst over the MacKay forces and their agreement with Orchard has always struck me as a little over the top, and as encouraged mostly by supporters of the losing candidates, which has been known to happen. The agreement with Orchard would end up meaning very little, as it outlawed a "merger" that would end up not being plausible or practicable in any event.

The MacKay victory was a significant step beyond the Clark era for the party. MacKay had been a child of the party in a riding not always easily held in Nova Scotia, and one that Tories would always need to hold to have any chance to win an election. He was elected leader with strong support in Quebec.

MacKay had been open in his campaign about the need to "unite the conservative family" to better fight the Liberals. The simple truth was that this would not be possible with older Mulroney-haters involved in the Alliance, and with at best indifference and at worst animosity toward both Quebec and the moderate strains of conservatism in urban and eastern Canada. The young leadership of the PC Party all knew that without a union with the Alliance on some constructive basis, the conservative alternative would be crushed by the coming unavoidable Martin onslaught. These leaders included the contingents of Dr. Kellie Leitch, Graham Fox, Dany Renauld, and Nova Scotian John MacDonnell; those associated with Percy Mockler in New Brunswick and with the constructive, middle-of-the-road Lynn Verge and Tom Marshall in Newfoundland; the Lougheed-tradition Tories in Alberta, such as Whitney Issik, Cynthia Moore, and Lee Richardson; and the Doug Emsley and Bill McKnight moderates in Saskatchewan.

MacKay would find common ground with this element in the party— and country—soon enough. In the Senate, BC's Gerry St. Germain had left the PC caucus to sit as an "Alliance" senator, the first in the upper chamber. Gerry was a former national president of the Progressive Conservatives, a Mulroney-era cabinet minister, a former pilot, cattle rancher, and building contractor. He had been both minister of state for transport and minister of forestry in the federal cabinet. St. Germain was a symbolic gain for the Alliance—becoming at once the first former Mulroney minister and Canadian of Métis origin (of which the senator has always been notably proud) to join the Alliance caucus. And he very much took Stephen Harper under his wing in parts of BC where he held great sway. St. Germain took great heat from his PC caucus colleagues in the Senate, but he was no shrinking violet. In 1998, he had the remarkable courage to support me when I sought the leadership against Clark.

In fact, in a sea of Orchard riding wins thought the Prairies, we were able to take the Prince George riding, in large measure because of the wonderful work of St. Germain's organizers such as the sage Byng Giraud and the simply remarkable Alex Kenyan. Gerry was an early adopter of the idea that we needed one conservative party, and it would surprise no one that his role in the process to come would underline that leadership.

11

The Alliance under Harper

In the March 20, 2002, race in which Stephen Harper took the Alliance leadership from Stockwell Day, Harper was the least likely of the candidates to embrace the fundamentalist school of mixing religion and politics. Day always made a clear distinction between his own religious views (he did not work on Sunday, the Christian Sabbath) and the public-policy views of the party ("I would never impose my religious beliefs on anyone else," he was fond of repeating, no doubt sincerely). Nevertheless, his initial victory over Preston Manning in July 2000 was powered not only by his telegenic attractiveness and dynamic personality, but by many individuals who joined the party because of their strong views, shared by Day, on abortion and other social-conservative issues.

Day even received support from some in other communities (Muslim,

Jewish, Sikh, Roman Catholic) who shared his innate conservatism on these sorts of questions. His undoing in the election of 2000, however, was a result not of this, but of the huge gap between the promise of his leadership—a dynamic, policy-based, clear alternative government with loads of new energy and competence—and a sophomoric, incompetent campaign. The latter was studded with bad logistics, policy the campaign could not explain, and the pervasive sense that his organization was not ready for prime time. No events better encapsulated the disconnect between promise and delivery than his visit to a home in southern Ontario to address tax cuts in a kitchen-table session—with the media in tow—only to find out that the wife in the family was leery about tax cuts. She was being treated for breast cancer at a regional hospital and did not want to see tax cuts that limited hospital funding. Day actually recovered quickly, with a rational and fair extemporaneous response about Alliance commitments to more health care funding, but he clearly had not been informed by his advance team. The Alliance commitment to more funding from Ottawa, to full reinstatement of the Martin cuts to provincial transfers, and to more provincial flexibility made solid policy sense. Ironically, it was precisely what the Martin federal government and the provinces would agree to in 2004, and what the Kirby multi-partisan Senate committee report would call for but a few months later. Sadly, however, the Alliance seemed utterly unable to articulate this nuanced approach when up against the traditional "who will protect universal health care?" narrative of the Liberals, the Bloc, the NDP, and the Progressive Conservatives. During the TV debate in English, Day was reduced—no doubt in frustration with his own campaign's failure on the health issue—to holding up a small cardboard sign that said "no-tier healthcare." One of the cardinal rules of television is that if a picture is allegedly an answer, then the obvious public reaction would be to ask,

"What is the question?" The only possible answer to this picture was, "But aren't they the party who was *for* two-tier health care?"

And that, combined with the movement of Tory seats in Quebec and the Atlantic provinces to the Liberals, was how a third modest Liberal majority was built. Yet it was a measure of just how much many Canadians wanted an alternative to the Liberals that the Alliance under Day increased its popular vote, increased its seat total with a modest breakthrough in Ontario (three seats), and pulled off a much stronger performance in Ontario and Quebec than the Progressive Conservatives under Clark. But the media frame for this result became the gap between promise and delivery on the Alliance side and Clark's rescue of the Tories from a near-death experience. For many Alliance members and MPs, the issue became, within that media perception, Day's allegedly erratic and unsustainable leadership style. In the onslaught that followed, the general perception of Harper shifted to see his thoughtfulness and intellectual groundedness as characteristics that would make him a solid leader. Harper's strong roots in the Manning (policy-wonk) wing of the party, his strong links with provincial conservatives nationwide—more deep and compelling in Ontario and the west than in the Maritimes—all added to his reach and appeal.

Several of Harper's characteristics and views earned him positive and interested media coverage on the ground: his privacy about his religious beliefs, his clear support (at that time) for individual free votes as opposed to party policy on the so-called social-conservative issues, and his openness to Quebec and strong advocacy for respecting sections 91 and 92 of the Constitution—that is, legitimately respecting provincial jurisdiction. And unlike Day, who was always up for some theatre and a good ten-second TV hit or front-page photo, Harper brought to his new role as leader three strong working principles: that he would avoid the contempt that undue familiarity with the media would bring to the "higher calling" of public office; that he would keep his private, religious, and public lives separate; and that he would not let political pressures diminish his priorities as an engaged father and husband, roles that were far more important to him than being a politician or even than getting elected. The media did not like his stance very much, but some in the press privately admitted to respecting Harper for it.

Moreover, since becoming leader, he had moved the party well away from the anti-immigration, anti-multiculturalism, xenophobic, and anti-Quebec traits that seemed, fairly or unfairly, to last through the Manning period of party ascendance and struggle. He also seemed much more comfortable with the separation between one's mission and world view as a Christian and one's role as a party leader and potential prime minister, a comfort that Manning was never able to achieve. It was not that people of faith and the strong views they had on abortion, same-sex marriage, capital punishment, or religion in the schools were unwelcome—far from it. It was simply that the Alliance as a party could not, as a collective, pluralist political force in the country, be a narrow vehicle for those views. Time and time again, Harper made the case, both during his leadership campaign and after his victory as Alliance chief, that letting these issues dominate party policy would seriously hobble the party and render it politically irrelevant.

In essence, Harper was narrowing the real gap in policy and intent between the Alliance under him and the Progressive Conservatives under Peter MacKay.

Both Harper and MacKay were of a different generation than Manning and Clark and, unlike them, were not caught up in the minutiae of decades-old and personal animosity, which they saw as having little to do with any definition of the public interest. Neither of them had been part of the old Stanfield-Trudeau rivalry—or the phenomenon of the Diefenbaker posse that so divided the Progressive Conservatives under Stanfield between 1967 and 1976. Neither of them had been part of the Blue Machine–Alberta battles that typified the Davis-Lougheed era, in which both emerging policy and federal party dominance were part of the mix. MacKay's father had given up his seat so that newly elected party leader Brian Mulroney could enter the House following his victory over Clark in 1983, and MacKay the younger was himself a Mulroney loyalist. Harper, in contrast, had of late made a clear distinction between the Mulroney the old Reform gang loved to vilify and the Mulroney of major policy achievements: free trade and undoing the Liberal National Energy Program. These were policies with which conservatives and westerners could identify. The Harper leadership was clearly a new opportunity for conservative forces to coalesce. At the very least, it was devoid of some of the previous sky-high roadblocks that had blocked any progress toward unity.

In fact, from Harper's point of view, various roadblocks had been replaced by directional signs that said that the road ahead was bumpy, but passable, including these:

- The Progressive Conservative Party, while possessing more seats in the House than in 1993, had a much smaller caucus than it had under Charest in 1997. Its ridings, financing, and internal organizational depth were, along with its popular vote, at the lowest point in its history. If Harper did not find a way to coalesce with the PC remnants, the federal Liberals under Paul Martin surely would, making perpetual Liberal majorities structurally unavoidable.

- Clark, who could not conceive of or support any new coming together of forces that he did not end up leading, was, mercifully, gone.

- Charest, whose championing of progressive Maritime, Quebec, and Ontario wings of the Progressive Conservatives might have been problematic, more in terms of colliding ambitions and careers, was wholly and fully engaged in Quebec provincial politics.

- Key financial forces on Bay Street, in Calgary, in Vancouver, and on Montreal's rue Saint-Jacques made it clear to both parties that it simply was not on to continue funding the kind of vote splitting that ensured continued unchallenged one-party government. While the Alliance under Harper was financially more solvent that the Progressive Conservatives that MacKay inherited from Clark, neither party was in great shape to muster, collect, or borrow the funds they would need to confront a centrist Martin Liberal party in 2004.

- Harper had won the Alliance leadership on the premise of stability, real policy alternatives, and competence. However, sustaining and leading the Alliance in another campaign with a split conservative vote in Ontario and a resurgent Liberal Party under Paul Martin would probably not see the Alliance's forces—or those of Harper—advance all that clearly. In fact, Martin was relatively popular in BC, Alberta, and Manitoba—important Alliance/Reform heartland areas that mattered a great deal.

Harper had been elected on the first ballot, overcoming a respectable field of Stockwell Day, Diane Ablonczy, and Grant Hill. All but one of those who had sat temporarily with Clark in the PC-DRC parliamentary coalition had returned to the Alliance fold, consolidating both the pro-Day and the anti-Day caucuses as loyal Harper caucus members. Harper had seen Clark step out of politics over the summer, with the dissolution of PC-DRC caucus bringing his second career as leader to an end. He had seen great white hopes for the Tory leadership, such as Bernard Lord, demur at the prospects of a fifth-place, technically bankrupt party with weakened leadership, a party reduced to a regional if feisty and determined parliamentary rump. He had seen MacKay, another young new voice, elected leader of the Progressive Conservatives, and Orchard theoretically remaining with real influence over the party's future, based on some kind of brokered convention arrangement.

Now it was June 2003. The Liberals would be choosing their leader in December or thereabouts. Martin could well seek a mandate from the people immediately. The prospect of another Alliance setback within seven to ten months was very real, as were some dire consequences for his own career.

The time to change the nature of the debate—and the conservative role—had clearly come. This was not about choosing to act or delay. It was about survival.

12

The Conservatives and MacKay

Peter MacKay's election as Tory leader at the end of May 2003 left the Tories precious little time to prepare for an election in which they would be facing a fight for survival against the Liberals in the Atlantic region, the Liberals and the Bloc in Quebec, the Alliance in non-urban Ontario, and the Liberals in the cities. Their prospects, except for a seat or two in Manitoba, were essentially non-existent west of the New Brunswick–Quebec border and under severe attack from the Liberals in many ridings. And they faced the popular Paul Martin, who had the support of moderate centrist conservative voters who were mildly nationalistic in Quebec, not ready for Alliance in the west, and tired of electing Conservatives in the Maritimes who could not deliver on federal largesse for their region or riding. This pretty well put the 13 per cent of the national electorate that Clark had bequeathed the party at risk. (If one assumes that the 13 per cent was actually 30 per cent or more in the Atlantic regions, it is clear how low it would have been elsewhere.) Despite his own boundless energy, MacKay faced some genuinely tough challenges:

- The Orchardistas could, if not in some way managed, seek to move the party toward a kind of nostalgic (and historically inaccurate) Diefenbaker agrarian anti-Americanism, one that could cut the party off from its pro–free trade, pro-defence, pro-alliance stance, reducing its support among core voters without in any way gleaning any new constituency of electoral value.
- His party was financially bereft, with too little traction or relevance in the business capitals to mount a campaign.
- While Jim Prentice was very much a team player, with a constituency and reach that made his support for the coming election both dependable and important, Scott Brison's petty Nova Scotia jealousy of MacKay made him unlikely to be dependable in the long run. Brison's leverage was now gone, and the likelihood of his rallying to the colours in any meaningful way was slim. He disliked MacKay intensely.
- The recruitment of first-rate candidates for Parliament would be most difficult, perhaps more so than at any other time in the party's history. There were no safe seats. Unlike the Bloc, Liberals, Alliance, and even the NDP, the Tories had no large or small bands of safe seats in various parts of the country. It is hard enough to recruit good people into the role of candidate for Parliament when one's party is a contender for government; when prospects are as challenging as they were for the federal Tories in the late spring of 2003, recruitment prospects are just about nil.

- Organizational talent had begun to drift to provincial conservatives in New Brunswick, Nova Scotia, and Newfoundland, and to Charest's "Liberals" in Quebec. It is a hard fact of politics that the best and the brightest and those who are building their own careers as organizers, policy people, staffers, and advance people gravitate to where the opportunities actually are. While MacKay had attracted a broad young cohort of supporters to the party, the talent balance was not working in his direction over time. Assembling the resources to mount a truly national campaign would have been the ultimate act of multiplying the loaves and fishes.

So the real prospect MacKay faced was that May 2003 was not one more election in which the party made progress but likely the last election ever for the party. It could likely, given the portents and a nearly certain increased Liberal majority under Martin, mean coming back with fewer than ten seats, no party status, Liberals in excess of two hundred, and the Alliance, Bloc, and NDP splitting the remaining ninety to one hundred seats.

In the midst of all this, MacKay was hearing a clarion call for reaching out to the Alliance and re-forming the old "Broad Church" Conservative Party from voices as disparate as Bernard Lord, Brian Mulroney, Mike Harris, Barbara McDougall, Don Mazankowski, Michael Wilson, Ernie Eves, Ralph Klein, former party presidents like Senator Gerry St. Germain of BC, Senator David Tkachuk from Saskatchewan, and many others. MacKay knew that Harper was, first and foremost, not Preston Manning or Stockwell Day. Harper now had in his parliamentary caucus MPs who had been part of the PC-DRC coalition. Coming to the side of finding a way to coexist or build a new conservative home for the two legacy parties were Chuck Strahl, with whom MacKay had worked closely, Tony Clement in Ontario, Dr. Kellie Leitch, and Peter Van Loan. MacKay's financial and organizational people were giving him the frank and hard news on the ground.

Meanwhile, Belinda Stronach, who had been a focused activist and financier behind the scenes for Conservative and Alliance leadership candidates and campaigns since 1998, was actively working to bring both sides together. As a corporate CEO and an active proponent of charitable and youth development projects (the "If I Were Prime Minister" university essay contest being among the most prominent), she had a large network across the country, especially for someone of her relative youth and political inexperience. What she may well have lacked in policy or grassroots experience she made up for at least partially with charm, intensity, and commitment. She believed that a One Conservative Party approach was the only alternative for a competitive Canadian democracy, and that a one-party state was unhealthy for the country. And she lacked neither impact nor clarity in making her case to both sides.

So MacKay faced a clear choice: take the safe route and defend the status quo, pray that the Alliance and the Liberals make a huge mistake, and hope for the best, or get the legacy parties together. The former would have been the path of least resistance for an Atlantic-region Tory, who, unlike Brison or Prentice, had not openly campaigned for merging with the other conservative party. But while that may well have been the safe choice, it would also have been the final choice for the Progressive Conservative Party. It clearly would allow both Martin and Harper to mop up whatever was left after the coming election.

The more difficult choice, but the right choice, was to find a way with a new, more centrist and receptive Alliance leader to see if something new could be built: a conservative party that brought the whole pre-1993 family back together—yes, with all its imperfections, but also with all its roots and linkages across Canada. It would not be an easy task, and it could be a task that would cost MacKay his recent and hard-won leadership. At the very least, setting aside the additive myth—the idea that one could add the votes of the two parties together (not true then, not true now), the existence of one national alternative government opposition party could give a reason to vote to those who did not want perpetual federal Liberal hegemony. And it would set aside the self-indulgence of ideological navel-gazing in favour of the duty to afford Canadians some option of substance in their electoral choices.

At the same time that MacKay was consulting broadly—including hearing from some members of former Ontario premier Bill Davis's caucus, Mulroney, and the rest—Harper, to his credit, was sending out signals of genuine openness to see what might be done. To be fair, Harper faced his own constraints, most significantly a party membership that had been seeking a de facto merger with the Progressive Conservatives for some years to no avail and that was running out of patience.

In May 2003, before MacKay was chosen leader, Harper's party had run hard against the PC candidate in the Perth-Wellington by-election; the PC candidate, Gary Schellenberger, became the fifteenth MP in the Tory caucus. As this was a heartland Alliance target zone in southwestern Ontario, the win, during a time when the party was essentially without a leader, indicated brand loyalty to the Progressive Conservative Party. This was probably enough to deny Harper's Alliance some traction outside the Prairies and BC. And just as MacKay faced a risk from the Orchard forces who were trying to pull the Tory party to the irrelevant left, so Harper faced the risk from elements of his own coalition who would gladly pull the Alliance into the barren fields of the equally irrelevant far right. While Harper's prospects of a credible first election campaign, possibly even becoming the official opposition, were better than those of the Progressive Conservatives, a party that starts as official opposition aspires to something better than the status quo. The Alliance was getting as good at leader change as the Tories.

So the months of June and July became a period of considerable back-and-forth between MacKay and Harper emissaries, diverse caucus personalities, various business leaders, including Stronach, and a host of former leaders, premiers, and senators. My own view at the time, though I had been quite removed from the partisan fray since 1998, was that the objective policy debate in the country required at least two political parties with the competence to form a national government. The centre/centre-left in the country had the Liberal Party of Canada; the critical public policy issue was whether the centre/centre-right would have a competent equally inclusive vehicle. Or would the slaughter of the innocents of 1993 be permitted to destroy democratic competition in perpetuity?

I made my own modest case on this imbalance in our national debate in newspaper op-eds and in speeches wherever possible, not so much as a partisan but as an observer from a public policy think tank, the Institute for Research on Public Policy. I liked MacKay and trusted his instincts and provenance and had supported his leadership bid. Harper had been a bright, thoughtful, and constructive member of the IRPP board when I joined the institute in 1999. I did not have to agree with him all the time to respect his intellect, sense of fairness, and articulate defence of thoughtful conservative policy choices. (The IRPP board was and is composed of a politically very diverse group of people with backgrounds that are Liberal, Conservative, NDP, social democrat, business, labour, academic, and public service, both domestic and international. The present chair, who succeeded Bob Rae when Rae decided to step down to seek the Liberal leadership, is Janice MacKinnon from Saskatchewan, a tough, able, and effective former minister of finance under Roy Romanow and a professor in Saskatoon.)

There would be factions in both parties that would deeply oppose any effort to reach out and build something new: the purists who believed that loyalty to the Progressive Conservative Party brand or to the more radical roots of Reform was more important than offering Canadians a viable national alternative. Many of these, such as Norman Atkins, Flora MacDonald, and Lowell Murray on the PC side, had long and distinguished histories of national and party service.

Yet the need to break the stalemate was underscored by the 2000 election result and the permanent default position occupied by the federal Liberals. There was a huge risk to both MacKay and Harper if they tried to build something new, but a much larger risk to the country if they did not.

13

A Family Reunion

The beginning of the summer of 2003 was the beginning of the last innings for the two young custodians of Canada's conservative cause.

Peter MacKay faced the prospects of an orderly Liberal Party transition to Paul Martin. The Liberal leader (and inevitable prime minister) was profoundly popular, particularly among moderate conservative voters in Ontario, BC, and the Prairies; he was even outpolling MacKay in the Atlantic region. MacKay had inherited a Progressive Conservative Party hobbled by almost five years of dithering, with no agenda, no policy, and little money—not the kind of prospects usually associated with attracting a stellar list of candidates. The prospect of a Martin romp through Quebec and Ontario, with Liberal seat pickups in the west and the Atlantic provinces and with the Alliance holding their strength did not portend well for the Tories' even managing to hold on to official party status. One more slip beneath those waves—1993 having been the first and 2000 having been the second near-drowning experience—would most probably mean the disappearance from the national scene of both the party and the brand of centre-right moderate politics it represented.

Harper, meanwhile, began the summer facing the same external political realities as MacKay, if from a somewhat stronger political base. A less than stellar electoral regional performance, with the other conservative party not part of the fold, would weaken his own grasp on the Alliance leadership. He faced the threat not of obliteration, but of stagnation and internal division. Reflecting the moderate and thoughtful Reform and Alliance stream, Harper clearly saw and articulated a difference between people of faith being involved in politics and matters of faith being dominant in politics. His tendency, if his history was any kind of guide, was going to be to confront a government on its record, extol a more confederal view of how the federation should work, and plump for less bureaucracy, less waste, more health investment, a stronger military, and lower taxes. These were mainline Conservative themes—he would leave the moral and religious skirmishes elsewhere. At the same time, he also understood, viscerally, the management challenge that this could represent and the degree to which two warring conservative parties could immeasurably advance the attractiveness of the Canadian voters' default position, which Martin was making even more convincingly logical than usual.

That kind of fractious election and massive Liberal outcome would only spell trouble for Harper and his more rationalist Straussian brand of conservatism, which is profoundly more intellectual than populist, far more philosophical than denominational. Furthermore, Harper understood, from Manning's formative tutelage and leadership of the Reform

Party, that control from the top—control of the riding lists and voting processes—was essential to sustaining the leadership capacity required for maintaining party coherence.

Both MacKay and Harper were hearing the growing chorus of rank-and-file members of their parties, along with more detached former leaders on both sides, who were eager for a coming together of one conservative party.

Mulroney had spoken in favour of this outcome, extending a hand of "let bygones be bygones" to his old Reform detractors. Manning had been on this track for some time. Clearly, active provincial conservatives—who, in Saskatchewan (in the Saskatchewan Party), Manitoba, and Alberta, were as often as not Reform/Alliance supporters, shared the Mulroney view. Premier Klein in Alberta had spoken often and expansively on this issue.

Moderates in the Progressive Conservative Party, such as former premier Davis, former foreign minister McDougall, and former finance minister and deputy prime minister Don Mazankowski, were also out in the marketplace of ideas calling for the family to be brought together. It was a view advanced by Premier Harris of Ontario and by leading Mulroney and Clark appointees to the Senate, such as Dave Tkachuk from Saskatchewan and Gerry St. Germain of BC (a former Conservative Party president), and the iconic Consiglio Di Nino, senator from Toronto. Activists in both parties at the riding level, especially among the youth federations and the fundraisers, called for a coming together.

Patrick Brown, who had been chair of my national youth effort when I ran for the leadership in 1998 against Clark, had been remarkably engaged on the issue. He had completed his law degree, was an elected municipal councillor in Barrie, Ontario, and was refreshingly outspoken on the need to pull the family together, taking Clark on publicly on several occasions for failing to reach out and, worse, for erecting barriers to the process. He spoke on many occasions for many younger activists and volunteers in the Ontario party who were frankly fed up with having to campaign against individuals federally whom they worked alongside provincially. It made no sense at all.

The business community was just about unanimous on the issue. Even hardline opponents of the Manning-era Reform Party, of which your humble servant was one, argued openly that, in terms of the competitive structure of the democratic electoral public-policy system, one coherent conservative party was now essential. In my case, I critiqued the "additive" argument that the 20 per cent of the Alliance added to the 15 to 20 per cent of the Tories meant 35 to 40 per cent for the new party, because it clearly would not, in any sustained or interregional way. What was important was the existence of a strong national party of the centre right with the clear potential to form a government and the rationale to attract people and develop policies to improve on what existed among the permanent governing large-L class of politicians, bureaucrats and business, and culture courtiers of the present establishment.

Both MacKay and Harper faced costs and consequences on both sides of the choice. Each had just gone through a leadership convention, with Harper also having just won election to the House. A genuine case could have been made to each that staying the course for one more election might be more prudent. The harsh reality for both of them, however, was that the risks of not uniting were even more powerful.

The decision of both leaders to tear down the Berlin Wall between the two parties and allow a group of statesmen from each side to begin discussions after July 2, 2003, was one of courage. In both caucuses and among their rank and file there would have been skeptical notes sounded. The notion of the process moving ahead without serious leaks or tantrums on either side would be hopelessly optimistic. But, in part, the individuals chosen for both sides were a clear indicator of how serious and sincere both sides actually were.

The Alliance team had three members, each of whom reflected a different strain in the party. Senator Gerry St. Germain was an interesting choice. A Conservative who had supported Mulroney for leader, been national president of the party, had chaired my campaign for leader in 1998 in BC, and had declared himself an Alliance senator while Clark was in his second leadership term. St. Germain was an unabashed apostle of one conservative party. His roots were in the Mulroney camp, the more moderate urban Tories who had worked on my campaign and a party network nationwide.

Ray Speaker was a prominent Alberta Tory minister in the Don Getty cabinet who had been a respected, fair, and distinguished part of the early Reform Party, having been elected in 1993 to the House of Commons. He also had a reputation for being discreet. Upon the leader of the opposition's nomination, he had been appointed by the prime minister to the Security Intelligence Review Committee, which is made up of privy councillors nominated by the parliamentary parties and which is responsible for oversight junction under the CSIS Act. These are by definition extremely serious and sensitive matters that require some very compelling levels of judgment and courage. Moreover, Speaker had links to vast strains of the Alliance nationally and to the Conservatives provincially in Alberta.

The appointment of Scott Reid (MP for Lanark–Frontenac–Lennox and Addington) to this band of emissaries spoke volumes about how closely and seriously Harper viewed these discussions. Intellectually, Reid is an integral part of Harper's brain trust. He is an individual of wide and pervasive reading and writing regarding the more small-c dynamics of the Reform/Alliance national mission. He asks tough (and sometimes not terribly politically correct) questions about axiomatic national truisms, such as official bilingualism, and maintains strong intellectual connections to think tanks. It would be difficult to think of a new idea, fresh policy departure, or policy rethink within Harper's Alliance of which Reid would not be an integral part. He is perceived to be close to Harper, both politically and conceptually, and, whether true or not, the perception affords constructive leverage.

The Progressive Conservative delegation had equal or even more convincing *gravitas*. William Davis, the premier emeritus of Ontario, was still for thousands of Conservatives and other Canadians the embodiment of fairness, balance, moderation, and courage in public life at their best. His presence at the negotiating table would be a comfort for the many who were angst-ridden over the risks of joining with the Alliance. Moreover, his agreement to any terms of union would reassure Tory moderates in the Senate and House, and the overall membership of the Progressive Conservative Party. MacKay's choice of Davis was inspired.

Few members of Mulroney's cabinet had been more vociferous about the Reform threat to the Tory base on the prairies than Don Mazankowski. He had been elected in the Stanfield era, had been the most senior of ministers in the Mulroney cabinet, and was a key part of the Conservative Party's soul in the west—in the good times and the bad. He connected deeply with federal and provincial parties, had friends in Reform, and was seen as one of those whose loyalty was to the party as a national institution. Despite an active business career on boards, he was still also involved in public-policy matters, having chaired a policy commission on health care for the Alberta government.

Loyola Hearn, the MP from Newfoundland, former cabinet minister in that province, and now House leader for the Tories, was a vital link between the discussions and the caucus. MacKay depended on him to maintain thematic coherence in committee, in question period, and, where possible, in substantive debate. Hearn had been part of the strategy to both accommodate the breakaway Alliance MPs under Clark and subsequently to coordinate in some measure between the two conservative parties in the House.

All six negotiators had linkages to and beyond the present leaders of their parties. Some had linkages of depth and substance in the provincial or federal wings of the Progressive Conservative Party. None had been tied to the more difficult attacks or counterattacks that typified the Manning, Day, Charest, or Clark periods of the prior decade. "Clean hands" in politics is often a euphemism for "out of the fray." The description did not apply to these six individuals, however; they were all the type of politicians to display dignity under stress and magnanimity in victory. Both qualities would be essential in the back-and-forth that the summer would involve.

The first face-to-face meeting did not transpire until August 21, although telephone consultations and exchanges of paper had begun before then. In the Conservative case, the emissaries knew that whatever could be worked out—if anything could—would be presented to the leader, to the PC management committee, to the national council, to the national caucus, and to a party-wide referendum. While both parties made it clear they would hold final referendums to ratify any agreement made, the Alliance interim stages prior to their referendum were less than clear. But from the first meeting, at a small inn in Mississauga not far from the airport, genuine progress was made. There were also setbacks, as when the Alliance appeared to be ending the process after a reasonably successful meeting on September 22, which had set a further meeting for September 29. The decision by Harper to end the process on September 27 was clearly a tactic to force the Tories' hand on the core and critical area of disagreement: how decisions both about transition to the new party and about subsequent choices on leader, policy, and constitution would be reached. The Tories stood steadfastly on the principle that every riding should have equal status; the Alliance felt that every party member should have equal status, with a one-person, one-vote approach. To be blunt, following this policy would mean that thirty thousand voters in Calgary could swamp the votes of an entire region like the Maritimes— and thus destroy any possibility of the two parties joining on an equal footing. The ability of one region (or, not to put too fine a point on it, one group of evangelical congregations) to swamp everything from a leadership process to a policy platform just would not wash.

The Alliance argument was not without some compelling points:

- The Alliance and Reform were populist parties of some standing, and the principle of one member, one vote had always been part of their history.
- A critical part of the party's broadly promoted populist narrative was the rank and file's control over critical party decisions. Losing this populist link would unfairly limit one of the party's clear advantages.
- One of the very best ways to broaden and increase membership

is if membership actually means something and has some clear prerogatives.

The Tories' response was also persuasive:

- Every riding in the country, however large or small, however many people vote on election day, results in one elected MP in the House of Commons. This is the core principle of our parliamentary democracy and basic to the operation of the Progressive Conservative Party historically.
- The absence of equality between the ridings would discourage the need for nationwide campaigns, either for leader or on policy issues; regionalism in the party and specifically in the west would be encouraged.
- Clearly, the Alliance had a larger membership in their western strongholds than Conservatives had in their Maritime, Quebec, or Ontario ridings. Allowing an unweighted membership vote, or even a delegate system tied to the amount of members each party had in any riding, would have relegated the Tory party to a wholly owned subsidiary of the Alliance. As the premise was two parties joining on an equal basis to create a new one, this simply would be a deal-breaker for MacKay and the Tory emissaries.

In the end, Harper—despite immense pressure from those who did want Calgary Alliance members to be in the driver's seat, and after some backing and forthing and a touch of brinksmanship on both sides—relented and accepted the Tory terms. This was an act of supreme statesmanship on his part, one that embraced a core principle of Canadian politics and public policy: that place is as important as pure numbers of people. In our federal system—in the core constitutional sinews of the Canada built by the Fathers of Confederation—where one was from and how one's region or province was treated were and are as important as any raw number count.

As not so much of an aside, in my graduate seminar at the Queen's School of Policy Studies dealing with how laws and governing instruments are chosen, shaped, and operated, I always make the point that while in many countries public-policy decisions are an amalgam of who, what, when, where, and why, in Canada the dominant variable and hot button is always where. Think fighter aircraft, frigate construction, health care policy, regional development agencies, highway investment, energy pricing and regulation, and location of federal and provincial ministries and Crown corporation head offices. Even the census-based design of our electoral map is only partially about some measure of equal population distribution per seat: Prince Edward Island has four seats with about the same total population as one riding in downtown Toronto or Vancouver. In terms of representation in the House of Commons, the average rural or small-town voter has much more clout than the average big-city voter.

There was much beyond this one salient disagreement that was agreed to remarkably and congenially by both groups of emissaries. But without this concession by Harper, we would still have two rag-tag political parties on the right as opposed to one potentially coherent governing alternative. It was that important.

The emissaries reached unanimous agreement on the following principles, summarized in the formal agreement and signed by both leaders:

- The two parties would treat each other as equal partners.

- The new Conservative Party would maintain ties with the provincial Progressive Conservative parties.
- Together they would create a national force that reaches out to all Canadians, not just like-minded conservatives.
- The new party would be guided in its constitutional framework and policy basis by the following policy principles and goals:
  1. A balance between fiscal accountability, progressive social policy, and individual rights and responsibilities.
  2. Building a national coalition of people who share these beliefs and who reflect the regional, cultural, and socio-economic diversity of Canada.
  3. Developing this coalition to mean embracing party and regional differences and respecting traditions yet honouring a concept of Canada as the greater sum of strong parts.
  4. A belief in loyalty to a sovereign and united Canada governed in accordance with the Constitution of Canada, the supremacy of democratic parliamentary institutions, and the rule of law.
  5. A belief in the equality of all Canadians.
  6. A belief in the freedom of the individual, including freedom of speech, worship, and assembly.
  7. A belief in our constitutional monarchy, the institutions of Parliament, and the democratic process.
  8. A belief in the federal system of government as the best expression of the diversity of our country, and in the desirability of strong provincial and territorial governments.
  9. A belief that the best guarantors of the prosperity and well-being of the people of Canada are: the freedom of individual Canadians

to pursue their enlightened and legitimate self-interest within a competitive economy; the freedom of individual Canadians to enjoy the fruits of their labour to the greatest possible extent; and the right to own property.

10. A belief that a responsible government must be fiscally prudent and should be limited to those responsibilities that cannot be discharged reasonably by the individual or others.

11. A belief that it is the responsibility of individuals to provide for themselves, their families, and their dependants, while recognizing that government must respond to those who require assistance and compassion.

12. A belief that the purpose of Canada as a nation state and of its government, guided by reflective and prudent leadership, is to create a climate wherein individual initiative is rewarded, excellence is pursued, security and privacy of the individual are provided, and prosperity is guaranteed by a free competitive market economy.

13. A belief that the quality of the environment is a vital part of our heritage, to be protected by each generation for the next.

14. A belief that Canada should accept its obligations among the nations of the world.

15. A belief that good responsible government is attentive to the people it represents and has representatives who at all times conduct themselves in an ethical manner and who display integrity, honesty, and concern for the best interest of all.

16. A belief that all Canadians should have reasonable access to high-quality health care, regardless of their ability to pay.

17. A belief that the greatest potential for achieving social and economic objectives is under a global trading regime that is free and fair.

Beyond these policy principles and goals, the emissaries embraced and agreed on these critical organizational and structural points, also included in the agreement and signed by both leaders:

- They would make every effort to marry the respective constitutions of the existing parties on the understanding that any points of contention would be addressed a future convention of the new party.
- The name of the new party would be Conservative Party of Canada. In adopting the name, emissaries fully supported the establishment of a partnership with all existing provincial Progressive Conservative parties and did not support the creation of any other conservative parties in these provinces.
- The Conservative Party of Canada would assume all the rights, assets, and liabilities of the Progressive Conservative Party of Canada (PC) and the Canadian Reform Conservative Alliance (CA). The parties would exchange financial statements to establish the present financial condition of each party for consideration by the membership.
- The CA and PC leaders would be responsible for achieving support of their parties for the goals and legal establishment of the Conservative Party of Canada as expeditiously as possible. (This produced executive-wide, riding-wide, and caucus-wide votes and two separate referendums, one in each party.)
- A critical path would be completed as soon as possible, and all necessary steps and timelines quickly detailed, given the pressures facing both parties in an election year.
- The CA and PC parties would determine the total number of members who would comprise an interim governing body, and each leader would then appoint an equal number of members to such a body. The

leaders would establish terms of reference for the interim governing body before the appointment of any members took place. The new interim body's priorities would be:

1. To ensure filing with Elections Canada (if appropriate and in accordance with Bill C-24).
2. To draft a constitution.
3. To establish electoral district associations.
4. To oversee candidate nominations.

- The new Conservative Party of Canada would immediately establish a trust capable of raising money and retiring the debt of either party. This entity would be the predecessor of Conservative Fund Canada. This would be subject to review by the appropriate party financial officials.
- The CA and PC parties would together determine the total number of individuals who would constitute a leadership election organizing committee, and the parties would then appoint an equal number of individuals to such a committee.
- The founding convention would be responsible for the amendment and adoption of a constitution and a statement of principles and policies. The PC emissaries indicated that the date and location were to be specified later.
- The system used to elect the next leader need not be used for later leadership elections, and the membership of the Conservative Party of Canada could select an alternative method for electing the leader in the future.

This was a remarkable agreement in principle. When initialled by MacKay and Harper at Ottawa's National Press Theatre in the fall, it was, in a very real sense, the dismantling of the Berlin Wall that had been erected by Manning brick by brick, and wire post by wire post, since the mid-1980s. It was a wall whose foundation was, to be fair, a sense in the west that only Quebec mattered—from the Constitution to procurement to everything else in between—that while Mulroney and the Tories had been sent to Ottawa to clean up the massive Trudeau-Turner deficit (it began under Finance Minister Turner in 1974), the total deficit actually got worse; that in spite of the long-time loyalty of western voters to the Tories for three long decades, from Diefenbaker in 1958 to Mulroney in 1988, genuine western concerns simply did not register, with the federal government taking a remarkably Quebec-friendly stance on most issues, in spite of the unprecedented western presence in the upper reaches of the cabinet and government (foreign affairs, finance, the deputy prime minister, transport, defence, agriculture—even the governor general came from the west). These issues included military initiatives such as deployment of troops to Iraq and the Gulf in the first Gulf War, free trade and NAFTA, and the Western Accord of 1985. (Ironically, I remember Conservatives in Ontario making the same comment, but being not terribly troubled about it.) Manning had built that wall with great expertise, on everything from refugee determination to the absence of a Triple-E Senate to a sense that Ottawa's policies excluded "people of faith" to the continuing nuisance effect of some of the hiring and promotion practices associated with aspects of official federal bilingualism.

While Progressive Conservatives would protest that under Mulroney the west had greater sway than ever, with posts like finance, deputy PM, transport, foreign affairs, defence, and forestry being in western hands, Manning had successfully build the opposite case—that it simply did not matter.

Manning's competence should not have been a surprise: he was an expert management consultant who had telling success at community and business development in many Prairie cities and communities, including the north and, as importantly, including First Nations communities. Furthermore, he had received solid policy help from Harper and was aided by absolutely compelling *vox populi* candidates for Parliament— Deborah Grey, Ray Speaker, Rahim Jaffer, John Reynolds, James Rajotte, Diane Ablonczy, and a host of others. His candidate lists were younger, more rooted in the business and community life of their cities and towns, and more multicultural and multiracial than Tory, Liberal, or NDP lists.

Manning also capitalized on a reality about western Canada often forgotten by political scientists and journalists who reflect on the more republican, small-c conservative nature of the prairie voter. While folks in the east think of the west in the context of Métis, Scottish, Irish, Ukrainian, Polish, German, and now South Asian populations and patterns of settlement, the truth is that the largest settlement around the turn of the last century was that of Americans coming north for affordable grazing land for their cattle. This, added to by the past half-century of oil and gas exploration, explains much about the cultural and political sensibilities of the region. Core ideas such as the need to have countervailing authorities in government to keep any one branch from being too powerful can be seen in the historical concern that each province have equal representation in the Senate or that judges be elected rather than appointed. These traditionally American patterns of political thought explain the Bible-belt evangelical reality on the Prairies in the post-Depression years—a tradition very much part of the home into which Preston Manning was born.

This deeply rooted suspicion of central government, of the eastern establishment, and of bureaucratic arrogance is an important part of our confederal political culture. While it is sometimes over the top, it is also often backed up with genuine reality. It is an honourable part of our political culture, and Manning knew how to exploit it, expand it, and erect a barrier between conservatives with it. But it is important for Tories and others to understand that it was not a movement only for those on the right. After the 1993 and 1997 elections, it became clear that this was not primarily an ideological vote on the far right, but a populist vote of anger and frustration, reflecting a strong sense of exclusion. This was clearly in evidence when solidly NDP provinces such as Manitoba and Saskatchewan voted Reform/Alliance federally. And to be fair to Manning, however well he built his side of the Berlin Wall, the Tories were no slouches in their workmanship on their side. Many Tories, including me, focused on the more anti-Quebec, anti-refugee, Christian fundamentalist strains of the movement and not only dismissed them as un-Canadian, but sought to diminish their relevance to the political mainstream. What became apparent after the second Manning election (and his last as leader) was that the movement was not a flash in the pan, but a legitimate and important expression of western anger and disengagement.

In the leadership campaign of 1998, only Brian Pallister, then a Manitoba Tory cabinet minister and now a leading MP from Portage la Prairie, Manitoba, and Michael Fortier, then a lawyer and subsequently a Quebec investment banker (and now Minister of Public Works and Government Services) spoke freely and plainly about the need to merge the two parties of the right. My final vote total was many times theirs, but they were well out ahead on the issue of uniting the conservative family.

While I was not as shrill as Clark back in 1998, I simply could not get beyond Manning and my sense that his new political family seemed unduly open to anti-gay, anti-immigrant, anti-Quebec voices, producing an unacceptable chauvinistic view of the country, never mind whether he ever embraced the view himself or simply knew that members of his coalition did. So I did my share to build this Berlin Wall by speaking only about reaching out to conservatives of all kinds to build a "working coalition on the centre right" for a better Canada.

But by the end of 1998, it was becoming clear to me, as I toured incessantly from riding to riding, how bereft of bodies the party was in large parts of the west. If Orchard had not flown in so many left-union Council of Canadians supporters to Edmonton for the all-candidates leadership debate, the hall would not have been full—and this in Clark's home province. Tory supporters were determined, young, engaged, and tiring of the internal fight in which they were on one side in federal elections in the west and on another side, with their federal Reform opponents, at provincial election time.

However high and tall the wall was between the two federal parties, little tunnels to freedom and unity were being dug underneath it during provincial elections in Ontario, Manitoba, Saskatchewan, and Alberta. But the hard truth remains that nothing would have produced any outcome at all if MacKay or Harper had blinked or chosen the easy path that summer and early fall of 2003—not speeches and private representations by Mulroney; not conversions to the cause of a unified party by great and eloquent personalities such as John Crosbie of Newfoundland; not engagement from premiers such as Filmon, Klein, or Harris; not determined lobbying by such Bay Street scions as Hal Jackman and Fred Eaton; not committed efforts by PCYF leaders such as Patrick Brown of Barrie and able strategists such as Leslie Noble and Tom Long; not genuine openness by prominent Quebec organizers such as Dany Renauld or Senator Pierre Claude Nolin; not the quiet advocacy of business leaders and organizers in the west, such as Doug Emsley in Saskatchewan and Rod Love in Alberta, or in the east, such as Belinda Stronach in Ontario. MacKay and Harper took the courageous step, a step more for Canada than for their own careers—a step more for political balance and the competitive democratic structure of the country than for their own immediate prospects.

They would be vilified for this move by some, and still are. But whatever else they may or may not do in our nation's politics, they deserve to be lionized for the agreement they came to and for the accord that their emissaries brokered and negotiated and that they each then took to their respective parties for broad referendum votes and debates. Think of what was accomplished in less time than most parties take to revise their constitution: the high voter turnout; the overwhelming yes votes in both parties, in excess of 90 per cent; the smooth melding of three hundred riding associations across Canada; the cobbling together of an interim organization and election committee and a new joint fundraising team, between November 2003 and the election in June 2004—not to mention the small matter of a leadership convention and contest pitting Harper against Stronach and the irrepressible and decent Tony Clement from Ontario. It was a Herculean feat for a newly minted opposition party. And what of the Liberals while this wall was coming down? They, of course, were preparing their anti–right-wing-extremist volley, in the event that the road to electoral coronation became in any way cluttered by the reality of a genuine democratic alternative.

PART 3

Regaining Relevance

14

INTO THE ELECTORAL FIRE

When the Tory side of the six wise emissaries reported to the party's national caucus, including senators, one of the saddest responses, despite the widespread support for what the emissaries had achieved, was the decision by two senators, Norman Atkins and Lowell Murray, to demur and become independent Progressive Conservatives. Atkins (a dear and trusted friend and associate for years) and Lowell Murray (while a resolute Campbell and Clark supporter in the leaderships of 1993 and 1998, nevertheless a significant intellectual and organizational force in the party) were, in the best of faith, letting the excellent become the enemy of the good. Both owned a large part of their prominence to Bill Davis's political success, to which Atkins had contributed substantially. During the momentary Clark government of 1979–80, it was Davis who agreed to Clark's appointment of Murray to the Senate from Ontario instead of from Murray's home province of Nova Scotia or from the place he had served as Richard Hatfield's cabinet secretary, New Brunswick. And Atkins had been the remarkably talented and tactically brilliant campaign manager for all of Davis's election victories—two tough minority wins and two compelling majorities. Atkins's appointment to the Senate not only reflected Mulroney's gracious recognition of his successful role as his campaign manager in 1984 and 1988, but also responded to polite but clear representations from Davis. The notion that either Murray or Atkins would walk away from the agreement brokered and negotiated with great care by, among others, Bill Davis, underscored one hard-core reality of the new political context. However successful the destruction of the wall between federal conservatives, however well both sides had bent to accommodate the other, however much a new generation of leadership could achieve what a previous generation could not from 1993 to 2003, there would always be individuals who retained an interest, a stake, a sense of self-definition in the old distinctions.

It's true that in the Stanfield Progressive Conservative Party, there were permanent gaps of substance between urbane Halifax and Toronto Tories and more conservative Tories in the rural west. Never mind that the conservative forces had been relevant and competitive only when left and right, urban and rural, east and west operated as one conservative party. There have always been and will always be tensions within a party more loyal to ideas than member to member. But it is the very existence of those tensions that make the party relevant. In contrast, the Liberals tend to submerge tensions on substance beneath tensions between warring elites, each desperate to grab the prize. Why, or for what policy goals, matters little.

And where was Clark in all this? There remained a genuine affinity for his view of the party—proved partly by the fact that senators Atkins and Murray could not embrace the same reconciliation that a Davis and Reid embraced, however uneasily, or that Hearn and St. Germain signed on for. In the months after the new party was forged, Clark would endorse the Liberals in two ridings, one in Nova Scotia and one in Alberta, and campaign for them in Edmonton, helping Anne MacLellan—a remarkable way for a former Conservative prime minister, foreign secretary, and party leader to end his political career. There is little reason to question Clark's sincerity, or that of Scott Brison who left the Tories to join the Liberals, or that of the above-mentioned senators. But Clark's actions, however witting or unwitting they were, helped create a line of attack that the Martin Liberals would use during the June 2004 campaign.

As always, the Liberals would be helped not by their own policy prowess or core coherence, but by the wilful disunity some in the Tory party seem unable to avoid. These Red Tory apostles of nostalgia would be aided, in their stand on the left, by individual Conservative members caught out on the far right during the campaign of May–June 2004, before the votes were counted on election day.

It is important, in trying to understand the significance of these divisive notes at the margins of what was a strong and united resolve to make things work across the entire new party, to reflect on the strands of coherence and cooperative endeavour that came together during the first leadership race of the new Conservative Party of Canada.

Harper began with a commanding lead based on hard work, no small part of which was having won the Alliance leadership across the country, overpowering Stockwell Day, just a few months earlier. He had a strong organization across the country among his own Alliance supporters and among prominent provincial Conservatives such as John Baird, Ontario's minister of energy and MPP for Nepean, and Michael Fortier in Quebec. In a leadership race in which he won on the first ballot with 55 per cent, beating the closest challenger, Belinda Stronach at 35 per cent and Tony Clement at 10 per cent, there had been very little doubt from the outset that he would win. Still, the dynamics of that race spoke volumes about the fault lines the new party would have to address.

Stronach, a determined, wealthy, and street-smart young woman with style and presence, entered the lists with no particular political history or experience in either the Progressive Conservative Party or the Alliance. She had been interested in public affairs and had taken a major role in community development, encouraging the young leadership part of Magna, the multi-billion-dollar company her remarkable father, Frank Stronach, had built from nothing more than a small machine shop on Davenport Road in Toronto. She played a major role in the Fair Enterprise Institute and, as mentioned earlier, in the "If I Were Prime Minister" national essay contest (now called The Next Great Prime Minister program) aimed at the brightest of the bright university students across Canada. And in Tory and Alliance leadership campaigns in recent years, both Magna corporately and Belinda Stronach individually had been generous supporters of candidates they wanted to encourage. All of this gave Belinda Stronach the opportunity to play a substantive encouraging role to both sides during the summer 2003 negotiations.

But the leap from that to seeking the top job in the new party caught many party members, including Stronach's friends and admirers, by surprise. Nevertheless, some organizational strengths, ample financial resources, and expert counsel saw her move from zero to 35 per cent in almost no time.

In Quebec and the Maritimes, her campaign handily overcame Harper's broad national profile and grassroots strength in Ontario and the west. John Laschinger, as her campaign chair, brought to her side perhaps the most concentrated level of expertise available at that time anywhere in the party. Mark Entwistle, a former Mulroney press aide, seconded from external affairs, joined her travelling staff. His career in External included stints as chargé in Moscow and Israel, and subsequently as ambassador to Cuba. Janet Ecker, a former Ontario finance minister, and Tom Trbovich, a former national director of the Progressive Conservative Party, joined on, as did Dany Renauld and his estimable, competent, well-rooted organization in Quebec.

Several senior players in the party were honourably attracted to Stronach's candidacy, not only for feminist reasons but because they saw her as a moderate, modern, and urbane force for what the new party could mean. These included Tories from John MacDonnell, PC president in Nova Scotia, to Senator David Angus, a long-time Maritime law specialist and fundraiser in Quebec for successive Tory leaders, to Barbara McDougall, Davis, Harris, and many of their respective entourages. My non-partisan professional life made participation inappropriate, but my personal support in the race went to Tony Clement. I felt that having a leader with cabinet experience and deep political roots in Ontario would be invaluable in the coming election, where Ontario would count for so much.

Harper campaigned along the high road and kept his campaign focused on policy and continuity—and made a key point of not letting issues of morality or faith-based concern become dominant. Stronach campaigned very much from the dynamic centre of the political spectrum, unabashedly defining herself as a new generation of leader on the basis of being an outsider from the private sector and a "live and let live" conservative on issues like abortion and same-sex marriage.

It should surprise no one that some sense of perspective was lost, given the hothouse atmosphere of the three hundred days between July 2003 and May 2004. But what was actually going on in the Tory leadership contest of 2004 was not just the resounding election of Harper to the leader's job—a job any observer could note he had earned and deserved—but the creation in Stronach of a proxy for the less conservative and more progressive wing of the new party. Very much to her credit, she took on this role without guile or negative history, making a virtue of the fact that she was not part of any Tory intellectual elite (which was usually self-anointed anyway) or that she was devoid of linkages to the Diefenbaker-Camp battles in the old Tory party or part of the building by both sides of the Berlin Wall in the 1990s. That she did all this with remarkable style and courage, despite so little experience, only made her candidacy all the more persuasive for so many. Meanwhile, the media missed the point, focusing instead on her fashionable and attractive platform presence, and various columnists showed their usual condescension. This spoke volumes again of how little her role in the normal tensions of a new conservative party was understood—perhaps, in its more profound implications, even by Stronach herself. What was more important here was not whether Stronach and her campaign team understood the salience of what she had come to symbolize, but whether *Harper* did. It was crystal clear from the polite acceptance speech by Harper, after his compelling first-ballot victory, that he did not.

Harper lacked no such nuanced judgment in preparing for the coming election campaign. Some have argued that he should have reached out to give campaign leadership roles to people such as John Laschinger, who had done such an outstanding job for Stronach and so many Conservative leaders and premiers before. The truth of the matter is that many of the same proponents would have argued that he should not desert the team that had seen him through this unbelievable political marathon, a thirty-six-month period in which he had won the leadership of the Alliance, negotiated the creation of a new political party with the leader of the Progressive Conservatives, fought and won a party-wide referendum within the Alliance in support of the merger, and then handily won the leadership of the new party. Moreover, I see no evidence from any source that Harper believed he was in anything other than the first part of a two-election strategy to unseat the Liberals. While his countenance on the first election night suggested disappointment, I doubt that at the outset of the election he though he had the remotest chance of even holding the Martin Liberals to a minority.

Certainly, from any structural sense, a more than acceptable goal would have been what he in fact did: build a competitive national alternative government—a strong Conservative opposition—that secured more seats than the two parties had in the previous Parliament. He ended up on election night with the largest Tory opposition since Stanfield elected 105 Tories to Trudeau's 107 Liberals in 1972. Yet two things transpired during the first two weeks of the campaign to set many party members' sights higher.

First, as is often the case when there is a remarkable national consensus on a Liberal romp, the media engaged to maximize any small government gaffe while the opposition parties got a free ride. In the lead-up to the 2004 election, the Martin Liberals did set a remarkable pace of small mistakes, everything from not being able to sort out a nomination in New Brunswick for Frank McKenna to appointing as Quebec lieutenant Jean Lapierre, who seemed unable to avoid any meadow muffins in the field of political comment and pontification. The marvellously outside-the-box promise-breaking first budget of the newly elected Ontario Liberal government was a further opportunity, as was the federal government's inexplicable "mad as hell" tour over the various allegations made by the auditor general about advertising and sponsorship contracts during the post-1995 referendum years in Quebec. From the outside, it looked very much as if the Martin brain trust had decided that the report was not an inherited political problem that needed to be dealt with but rather a rare opportunity to differentiate Martin and his new administration from Chrétien and his administration. This had the effect of shifting their campaign back from their classic ballot questions "Who will speak for Canada?" or "Who is more competent to govern?" to "Do you still trust the Liberals?"

Something that was quite un-Liberal happened in the way Chrétien left politics and Martin's troops took control of the party, resulting in Martin's ultimate ascendancy. There was, in a sense, a new standard of internal meanness set by both sides at various points through Chrétien's 1990 leadership victory in Calgary, the Liberal victory in 1993, and the ensuing decade. One would, even in non-partisan or Tory circles, pick up snippets of the intensity of the battle within Liberal ranks, even when the Liberals were truly and firmly on plan.

Chrétien had never forgiven Martin for the post-1990 leadership convention view in Quebec that Chrétien was not a "true son of Quebec" fighting the intellectual battle for Quebec particularity. Martin had been pro–Meech Lake and pro–Charlottetown Accord, while Chrétien had been, at best, lukewarm. In the transition to leader, Martin had not reached out to the vanquished as others had done in the past; they were broadly dismissed or sent to foreign posts, or they resigned from public life.

A Liberal Party unreconciled is explosive. Martin supporters who could correctly argue that they were outsiders during the Chrétien reign could not get over the fact that their man had been finance minister—and the second most powerful minister of the Crown.

Second, the unexpected Liberal win provincially in Ontario, under Dalton McGuinty, set up what is often a precursor of gains for the other party in federally—the Ontario voters' usual tilt toward balance and away from concentrating too much federal and provincial power in the same hands.

All of this played at first into and then out of Harper's hands. At the outset, the obviously honest, stable, and trustworthy Harper, looking very much the solid and dependable Tory (without any government experience that might reveal a skeleton or two), became the absolute proxy for a new and honourable point of departure for the country. Martin's inevitable lead as "best person to be prime minister" began to narrow from day one. The prime minister's 2004 tour early acquired a chaotic feel, smacking more of promise-a-day desperation than of surefooted Liberal competence. The attack on Liberal ethics advanced by Harper was aided by more pointed attacks from the Bloc Québécois (their slogan being "*un parti propre pour Québec*," that is, both Quebec's "own party" and a "clean party" for Quebec) devastated Liberals in Quebec. Martin's Quebec lieutenant, Jean Lapierre, who had a genuine following as a no-holds-barred political commentator, found himself commenting negatively on his own party's prospects in the province. Beginning to look at least as compelling as the early transitional cabinet Martin had assembled were strong Conservative candidates such as Lee Richardson in Calgary; Inky Mark, Vic Toews, and Brian Pallister in Manitoba; Peter Van Loan, Belinda Stronach, Bev Oda, John Baird, and Tony Clement in Ontario; and MacKay and a host of other strong candidates in the Maritimes, such as Dick Doyle and Loyola Hearn in Newfoundland, Bill Casey in Nova Scotia, and Greg Thompson in New Brunswick. All had experience and standing. Martin's transitional cabinet, in contrast, was remarkably nondescript. Martin failed to do what Trudeau, Davis, and Mulroney had done: reach out to their strongest rivals and bring them in, and in close (witness Mulroney with Clark, Crosbie, and Wilson—all of whom, except Clark, became powerful loyalists—as was the case with Davis and Darcy McKeough, Al Lawrence, Bob Welsh, and Bert Lawrence). All of the strong lights of the Chrétien era and all of the potential rivals to Martin (Manley, Rock, Tobin, and McKenna) were clearly not in the cards for Martin's cabinet team. This removed from them and their entourages across the country any stake in the 2004 election outcome.

Two strategically significant things happened after the first two and a half weeks of the campaign. First, the steady creep up the polls by the Tories from the mid-20s to the high 20s and very low 30s forced the media to begin to look at what a Tory government might actually stand for. Second, the Liberal numbers were artificially depressed by NDP and Bloc gains in various parts of the country. (Ed Broadbent was running for the NDP in downtown Ottawa, and Gilles Duceppe was performing well in every forum.)

When the Liberals moved in desperation to the "Tories as right-wing extremist" ads, expertly crafted by old Liberal stalwart and Red Leaf guru Jack Fleischmann (Red Leaf was the ad hoc group of agency executives from the advertising industry that coalesced every election to craft Liberal advertising), making audacious and factually not quite correct allegations about Tory defence (or "go to war in Iraq") policies, there was little Tory response. The ad campaign seemed to gain credibility when several Conservative MPs, including Randy White of BC, were associated with statements on abortion and the Charter of Rights. Although Harper had been the pro-choice candidate when he beat Stockwell Day for the Alliance leadership, he was not rapid and clear in his response to this development. The lack of clarity on abortion produced a serious collapse among female voters, first, and a further reduction among Quebeckers, who had been increasingly, in moderate numbers, considering the Tories. Finally, an over-the-top staff member crafted a media release suggesting that the prime minister was soft on child pornography, which required— and got—an eventual apology. The slowness of the response on the child porn mistake raised judgment issues.

While Harper performed well in the TV debate, both in form and in substance, Prime Minister Martin held his own in a determined and feisty way. What had been a trickle of a trend toward the opposition parties generally and the Tories specifically began to reverse in the last week. It is not clear that the Conservatives' own polling caught it, as expectations in that camp for a positive seat margin in their favour persisted right through election day.

All that being said, the Tories under Harper came through the fire of both the leadership and the election in remarkably solid shape. The Liberals had been reduced to a minority, made even more precarious by the fact that even when their votes were combined with the NDP vote, there was still no working majority in the House. The Tories had won twenty-four seats in Ontario, a breakthrough neither the Alliance nor the Progressive Conservatives could have achieved on their own, while holding or increasing strength in the west, especially Saskatchewan and BC. The effectiveness of the Liberal counterattack in the latter part of the campaign and the intensity and pace of the prime minister's own campaign in the last two weeks clearly helped save the Liberal government. But a ninety-nine-seat Tory opposition at the centre of a minority parliament was wildly beyond what either MacKay or Harper could have aspired to just twelve months earlier, when the Conservative Party of Canada did not even exist.

There was much accomplishment and transformative progress from which Canadian conservatives in general and Harper in particular could take quiet pride and satisfaction. The Conservative Party, as a national competitive force, was back as a real combatant in national politics. One major leg of the journey from the abyss of 1993 had been completed.

15

Minority, Discipline, and Choice

The wonderful reality of a minority parliament is that there is no apparent four- or five-year hiatus during which any meaningful planning on policy or tactics can take place. That said, the current minority Conservative government has followed, in short order, that party's stint as opposition to the Liberal minority government. The challenges and choices of such parliamentary situations are worth reflecting on, especially considering that the Conservative Party seems to have learned, for the good of its current minority situation, from the mistakes made by Martin in his first minority.

First of all, the campaign run by Harper and his aides in 2005 and 2006, culminating in the January 23, 2006, victory, was remarkable for its simplicity, discipline, and focus. Harper treated voters with respect, regularly and frequently putting on the table solid policy proposals based firmly on the broad conclusions of the March 2005 policy conference in Montreal. And, by and large, on the throne speech, budget, and accountability legislation central to his priorities, Harper—while not caving to opposition pressure—has been far more collegial than Martin was in the 2004 Liberal minority.

Minority parliaments lurch from real to pretend crisis on a weekly or daily, if not hourly, basis. Everyone is always busy. Because these minority parliaments tend to occur after long periods of domination by one party, the media are understandably taken up with the crisis atmosphere. If previous minority parliaments are an indicator, there are two parts to the public interest cycle. At the outset, there is genuine interest in the jockeying for position; the way each leader and party adapts to this changed, diminished, or heightened status; and the dynamics of the short-term changes and crisis. After a period of brinksmanship and crisis, a parliament then typically settles into its more generic cycle.

The outset of the parliament elected in June 2004 was made even more crisis-prone because of the testimony before the Gomery Commission addressing the Adscam advertising issues raised two years earlier by the auditor general, a problem inherited by Prime Minister Martin. The ease with which uncorroborated testimony was confused with truth or honesty by all players in the House—and, most surprisingly, by the media—was absolutely breathtaking. But that confusion actually produced the best of all circumstances for the Martin administration. The official opposition and the Bloc, for much of the session, were utterly incapable of resisting taking every bleat and bump from Gomery testimony into the substance of their day-to-day presence in the House. To be fair to both the leader of the opposition and the leader of the Bloc Québécois, the media and the public most likely would have been troubled if these leaders had not shown outrage and shock at some of the testimony. Nevertheless, the obsession over these "revelations" was inexcusable at a time when the country was beset with serious structural challenges on U.S. relations, defence policy, equalization, health care, trade adjustment, and resource management. In effect, the Adscam follies provided both sides with real cover and with ample opportunity to avoid policy clarity.

Avoiding policy clarity is one of the great tactics of political party planning, and the lessons from history are by no means clear on its effectiveness. One could argue that the Harris Tories in Ontario moved from third place to victory in the 1995 provincial election because they had put out a clear, grassroots-based policy document, "The Common Sense Revolution," a year or so before the election. This argument holds that this clarity and credibility, combined with Liberal incompetence (the Liberals squandered a 30 per cent lead over the Bob Rae New Democrats), produced the Tory victory. Yet Stanfield's 1974 position on a price and wage freeze, released before the campaign, arguably contributed to Trudeau's regained majority in the election of that year. While Chrétien's Red Book of 1993 (jointly crafted by Martin and senior policy adviser Chaviva Hosek) was an appropriate anchor to Liberal credibility and balance in that campaign, was it of any greater value than the collapse of Kim Campbell's campaign?

Did Davis regain his majority in 1981 because of the economic and social-development policies of the Board of Industrial Leadership and Development, as those of us who worked on them and their release long before the election believe? Or did the overall competence and attractiveness of the Davis administration and of the premier himself simply outflank the new NDP and Liberal leaders facing the campaign in 1981?

The new Conservative Party did not get a complete pass on substantive policy development or commitment. In fact, it was called on to reflect on two areas of challenge as it prepared for the inevitable Liberal-Tory electoral duel that would come within months.

The first challenge was restraining the troubling tendency, both unjustified and rarely productive of any electoral gain, to attack one's opponent as personally corrupt. The general notion that Paul Martin set aside his role as CEO of Canada Steamship Lines to run in 1988 in an election the Tories were widely expected to win and did so to enrich himself rather than to serve his country and party was both without substance and beneath its purveyors. The intensity of the Conservative focus on this particular line—in which caucus leadership was prominent—was unbecoming. Canadians may well believe that individuals associated loosely or otherwise with the Liberal Party in Quebec are perhaps guilty of fraud, violations of the election expense rules, and maybe even stealing from the government and the Liberal Party, with the accuracy of those beliefs either borne out or not by Mr. Justice Gomery's final report and/or criminal proceedings in the courts. But there is no evidence that Canadians believe, or have reason to believe, that Martin sought in any way or at any time to enrich himself in the process. When the Tories, in particular, went down this road—by attacking either Martin or those who supplied services to the Finance Ministry when he was finance minister, especially when those suppliers had provided similar advice and counsel to the previous Tory regime, they were engaging in a form of McCarthyism that degrades the whole system.

Further to this, Canada seems to have begun the rather sad tradition in which each administration alleges that its predecessor was corrupt. Mulroney was subjected to the worst and most venal allegations, utterly without any apparent substance, on the Airbus affair under Chrétien. Martin, in his "mad as hell" tour relative to Adscam, unwittingly unleashed a similar implication relative to aspects of the Chrétien time in office. The question was, would MacKay and Harper now engage in doing the same to Martin? Certainly, an election campaign in May 2005 based on a "we are honest, they are crooks" narrative could not have advanced the Tory cause. Ironically, Belinda Stronach's decision to leave the Tories and join the Martin campaign spared the Tories this kind of negative and likely unsuccessful electoral foray.

The election campaign that did not happen in May 2005, in some measure because of Ms. Stronach's defection to the Liberals, may well have been one in which the Conservative narrative would simply have been, "We are honest and they are corrupt." First of all, as a campaign posture for the Tories, this may have been sustainable for a week, maybe two. But in the context of an election in which the parties were coming out of a minority parliament, the pressure on the Tories to reveal their policy priorities would have been justifiably intense. The "who is more corrupt" narrative would have quickly become the "whose policies can you trust" narrative—which was the ballot question that kept the Tories out of power in June 2004.

So the focus on corruption gave the Liberals a remarkable respite from facing any real, competitive public-policy debate. It was unlikely, if history is our guide, that Canadian voters would have a strong preference for either the Liberals or the Conservatives on the issue of integrity in government. A Tory focus on this issue, as the 2004 election told us, was of immense value to the Liberals in general and to Prime Minister Martin in particular. It afforded the Liberals immense running room on policy and on ersatz coalitions with the NDP, issue by carefully polled issue. It gave them comfort in the knowledge that a coherent policy critique or competing initiative was relatively unlikely. The Tories, by focusing on scandal, were actually giving away all these tactical and policy options to the other side.

The second was countering the seeming Conservative incapacity to separate marginal from central issues. It is in the nature of a minority parliament that small issues become large and large issues get moved to the side. However, the Conservatives risked accelerating this process to their own political detriment. On the serious structural questions mentioned above, there was little substantive Conservative engagement. In fact, on the Canada-U.S. missile defence issue, the Conservatives were expected to take the traditional Conservative position of supporting continual cooperation in every way. But the Tories demurred when they could have at least simply proposed to engage cooperatively in North American defence.

Let's see what would happen, strategically, if this issue were played a different way. A Conservative position, clearly articulated before the prime minister's decision to stay out of missile defence, to the extent that any reasonable resolution before the House on missile defence would receive Tory approval, would have put Prime Minister Martin in a more difficult position between the Americans, the NDP, and the Bloc than did elements of his own caucus. The excuse that some Liberal MPs might oppose missile defence would have been trumped by the necessary Tory votes in the House to pass a supportive motion. By avoiding any such policy commitment, the Tories afforded the PM an exit route. This was difficult for the Americans to understand but was clearly explainable relative to uncertainty over Tory posture in the House. No doubt Ontario Tories were less than resolute on the matter and Harper was endeavouring to be accommodating, but the strategic implications were and are substantive.

The tactic of forcing an election—lustily played by Harper and his forces in May 2005—is part of the psychology of outrage a leader of the opposition either cannot avoid or must willingly embrace when the dynamic of public outrage is in his or her favour. However, the central theme in forcing an election in a minority parliament must be the opposition's plan for governing. And this plan had better be, in terms of policy priorities and public-policy goals, substantively better than that offered by the actual government and whoever is supporting them.

The Harper forces also stumbled in 2004 in allowing the same-sex marriage issue to expand from one on which all MPs would be allowed a free vote to one on which the Conservative leader made legislation on the issue his stated priority upon forming a government. This, too, was a case of letting the marginal overtake the substantive, at the expense of the party's broad credibility.

It is not that the issue was not of compelling importance as a matter of principle—on both sides of the issue. Harper genuinely tried to find a fair compromise by separating the notions of civil union with full legal rights for all couples, gay or straight, from the formal term *marriage*. However, every second he spent on this issue was one not spent on health, or taxes, or defence, or Canada-U.S. relations. This was about a case of letting the marginalia—same-sex marriage, which may be germane to half of the 10 per cent of our fellow Canadians who are gay—overcome the core issues of our time. The controversy played into the government's hands. All the government had to do was to look holier than thou in supporting the Supreme Court's interpretation of the Charter of Rights and Freedoms, playing to its constituency, which supported its stand on the issue—the constituency Harper needed to take: the vast majority of women, the vast majority of Quebeckers, the vast majority of Canadians living in our large cities. The 2004 parliamentary context would have to be sorted out by an election in which a majority government was either chosen explicitly or in which two like-minded parties had sufficient capacity and seats between them to govern for a considerable period of time. To be on the winning side of that electoral shootout, Conservatives needed to start assembling the key elements of the Harper Conservative coalition. And that coalition could not exclude 80 per cent of female voters, 80 per cent of voters under thirty, 90 per cent of Quebeckers and French-speaking Canadians, and the vast majority of visible minority, urban, and lower-middle-income Canadians.

There was also, beyond the substantive policy questions, a core strategic question Harper could not avoid. When Harris won the provincial election on 1995 in Ontario, many were of the view that his strategy—a "wedge" strategy, in which welfare and taxes were used as proxies to pull soft Liberals from the Liberals' incompetent campaign in order to afford the Tories a plurality of votes and a majority of seats—was the right one for the political times. It was certainly different from the big tent approach taken by Conservatives in Ontario such as Robarts and Davis. Neocons in the United States and some of their apostles in Canada have embraced this approach because a wedge vote can sometimes be "harder" and more likely to show up than a softer but broader big tent voting target.

Examining Prime Minister Martin's strategy in 2004, we can see that he clearly began with a big tent strategy but had to narrow his sights on the centre-left vote in the country by evoking the spectre of a narrow Conservative far-right administration, a strategy that was then heightened in the 2005 election.

In order to make the right choice in terms of both strategy and tactics, Conservatives had, and have to, come to terms with one key question: Are we prepared to lose votes and parts of our coalition in rural and western Canada in order to win massively more seats in Ontario, Quebec, and the Atlantic? This is not an easy question to answer for a party deeply rooted in the regional frustrations and grievances of western and small-town Canada, yet it is one that every Conservative leader must address. Stanfield addressed it by supporting official bilingualism in 1972, bringing him thirty seats closer to the Liberals and within one seat of their defeat. Mulroney faced it when he championed official bilingualism in Manitoba before the 1984 federal election, when even his local Tory minister, Jake Epp, lacked the courage to do so. In fact, Mulroney went to Manitoba precisely to do this, despite local political ambivalence and hostility. It is not an easy choice—it is much harder than the facile choice to oppose government corruption, whether real or exaggerated. But failure to make that choice makes shaping one's policy framework and overall public coalition strategy almost impossible, which in time may fatally harm one's party and personal prospects.

When the Conservatives met in Montreal in March 2005 for their first annual and general meeting since the genesis of the new Conservative Party in the fall of 2003, Harper went a very long way, along with the party rank and file, to addressing large parts of this core issue. The debates and votes on a range of questions produced decisions that were broadly based—responsibly conservative, but very much of the mainstream. The dropping of abortion from the platform, under Harper's clear leadership, was a giant step forward. Other decisions taken, from defence to bilingualism, from health to agriculture, were mainstream and fair-minded. Even the vote to retain the traditional definition of marriage while allowing for an equality-based civil union was likely to have been the same even if taken in the old Progressive Conservative Party. The critical choice now was how these votes would be treated, and how future platforms were to be shaped—what decisions about priorities, issues at the margin, and issues at the core of the party's offering to Canadians would be made by the leader and the campaign staff.

There was a danger that to conserve every one of its ninety-nine seats, the new Tories would not take the leap necessary to grow more into a mainstream conservative party, as opposed to a newly assembled derivative party. This was critical, because Canadians will not elect a government that appears to be based on a derivative composite of two other parties.

Not only was progress made on a coherent broad policy statement from the Conservative Party, with broad public support within the rank and file, but leadership on the part of Peter MacKay, John Reynolds, and Harper also kept a fresh rift from developing along the precise fault lines that had almost ended the negotiations between the old Alliance and Progressive Conservatives. MP Scott Reid proposed that key votes in the party go back to a one-person, one-vote structure and away from the equal number of delegates per riding approach agreed to in the agreement signed between Harper and MacKay. This matter came up as a proposed constitutional amendment for the new party at its March 2005 general meeting in Montreal.

MacKay engaged the issue directly, and moderates in the party, plus supporters from rural and smaller city riding associations, lined up in support. The young Conservatives, already bristling over the confirmed opposition of senior HQ leadership to a separate youth or student federation—a feature of the old Tory party (having developed Tories such as Ted Rogers, Hal Jackman, John Tory, Bill Davis, Roy McMurtry, Graham Scott, Barbara McDougall, Davey Fulton, and Brian Mulroney)—threw their support behind MacKay's stand.

To his credit, John Reynolds, campaign co-chair, was vocal in support of the original "all ridings equal" agreement. What could have been a messy fight, with the risk of affecting the confidence vote in the leader (which Harper carried handily), was averted in large measure because Reynolds and Harper put party unity first and MacKay had the courage to defend the integrity of the agreement upon which the "yes" votes in each of the legacy parties had been won in support of creating the new party.

The challenge of making the new Conservative Party real was begun at the March policy convention, but that was only a beginning, to Harper's credit.

While this reconciliation and family-building exercise was happening in the Conservative Party, the Martin-Chrétien dispute in the Liberal Party was only becoming deeper and more visceral.

16

Back on the Hustings

When Prime Minister Martin surprisingly appointed me to the Senate in August of 2005, and when I swore my oath of allegiance to the Crown on September 29, 2005, I was not sure what I might find in Ottawa upon arrival.

My network and my friends had always included people active within party circles, but I took very seriously my role as president of the Institute for Research on Public Policy, a profoundly non-partisan organization. I took no role in the 2004 election and had offered only informally solicited advice to Davis during the summer 2003 negotiations between the two parties. While I had been asked by Peter MacKay to be one of the negotiators on the Tory side, both Bob Rae and I (Rae being my boss and board chair at the IRPP) agreed that doing so would be too partisan a role for an IRPP president to play. However, when before the 2004 election I was asked by Stephen Harper to undertake transitional planning in the event of a Tory government, the IRPP board graciously agreed that this would be appropriate. In this role, I worked with Ambassador Derek Burney, Tom Flanagan, Graham Fox, and my indefatigable administrative assistant, Cathy Cavaglia. But beyond that, I was detached from the day-to-day party processes outside of what I read in the papers and observed on the news.

When Belinda Stronach defected to the Liberals in May 2005, propping up their frail government, I felt she had unwittingly done Harper a favour. The Tories did not appear ready for or in the right mindset about an urgent election call in May or June. While her departure was a loss, the unstable nature of her comportment within the Tory party likely meant that she could have left on any issue or at any time—for instance, more destructively, before the leaders' debate in the 2005 or 2006 election. In denying Harper an election in spring 2005, she probably denied Martin an enhanced Liberal minority or de facto majority and gave the Tories under Harper more valuable time to plan, organize, recruit, and raise funds, while the Liberals used their extra time to make some serious mistakes.

None of this could have been known at the time, but when I was interviewed on various television panels or all-news shows about the coming vote, my view that it was not in the Tories' interest to force an election that June produced the usual attacks on me in the various far-right wing websites and neocon blogs—further confirmation, if one ever needed it, of the appropriateness of my fears at the time.

When called by Prime Minister Martin for the Senate in late July, I had the option of sitting as an independent, a Progressive Conservative (with my old friends Lowell Murray and Norman Atkins), or a Conservative.

While I knew that sitting as a Conservative would disqualify me from continuing at the IRPP (a job and organization I truly loved and believed in) and that some of my old Tory friends would be surprised at my joining the Conservative caucus, my decision was immediate and resolute, and I tendered my resignation to the IRPP board at their earliest convenience. I would sit as a Conservative in the Senate and support Harper and the party every way I could.

The issue was crystal clear for me in many ways: First, Harper had made the gesture to bring the two old parties around the table, and had reached out to urban, eastern, and Red Tories to do so, not in his interest, but in the interest of a competitive democracy in Canada. Second, in all my discussions with Harper when I was at the IRPP (he sat on the board before I arrived), his integrity and candour were absolutely exemplary. Third, the only future for a viable national Conservative option to strengthen our national politics or improve the quality and sensitivity of government is vested utterly in the success of a national Conservative party that embraces its broad membership along the "rational conservative spectrum," which includes paleo-conservatives like myself, Red Tories, social conservatives, historical conservatives, and even the more flinty-eyed neoconservatives. A spectrum less embracing means uninterrupted Liberal hegemony in perpetuity, which would also mean the gradual end of competitive democracy.

I called Harper to give him a heads-up before the announcement was made by the PMO. True to his own views on the Senate (and to my own, which I still hold, having run on them against Clark for the Tory leadership in 1998), Harper welcomed me personally but underlined the party's commitment to Senate reform, a commitment I freely endorsed in my initial speech to the Senate on November 15, 2005.

What I found when I attended caucus was quite remarkable, and indicated just how much had been learned since the 2004 election. The caucus was disciplined and mutually respectful; members could express their views on bills before the leader expressed his; an open show of hands was used on several issues. The shadow cabinet and the leader's advisers were diligently working away on critical policy priorities for the campaign. The fundraising efforts of the new Conservative Party under the remarkable Irving Gerstein were making immense progress, positioning the party to benefit the most from new rules that limited corporate and union donations. The linkage between the Senate caucus and the caucus as a whole seemed close and well managed. The opposition leader in the Senate, Noël Kinsella (a former head of the New Brunswick Human Rights Commission under Premier Hatfield and appointed to the Senate by Prime Minister Mulroney), assisted steadfastly by House Leader Dave Tkachuk (Saskatchewan), Chief Whip Marjorie LeBreton (Ontario), and Deputy Leader Terry Stratton (Manitoba), reported regularly to the national caucus. The Senate caucus, while always more independently minded, was well linked to main caucus strategy. Certainly, the animosities that had existed in the past between the caucuses of the two chambers seemed to have passed.

So the net impression, both from his presence in caucus and the House, was that Harper was very much at peace with himself, refreshingly even-handed about his choices, and utterly unconcerned about media attacks or so-called collapsing polls. But the media bias was that a Martin win, with either an enhanced minority or a new majority, was inevitable. Media folk were largely respectful but dismissive of Harper's chances.

Shortly after taking my seat in the Senate at the end of September 2005, I was called on to address the breakfast club of the Ottawa Centre Tories at the National Press Club on October 5, 2005. Here is what I said, after scrambled eggs and bacon:

> There are three words I want to begin with this morning, three words that should focus our efforts as Conservatives and underline our core mission. They are simple, direct, and full of promise . . . and we must keep them at the centre of our work, together, as Conservatives. And they are: PRIME MINISTER HARPER.
>
> They are three words that encapsulate our core duty to Canada and to each other. They reflect the best possible chance for economic and social progress Canada and Canadians share. And they represent the very best option for change that we, as Canadians from coast to coast, can collectively embrace.
>
> Now, we need to accept that there are forces that are opposed to change. There are people who believe that after almost thirteen years of government by one party, one finance minister, one view of the country, change would simply get in the way. These people are what we call hard-core partisan Liberals. They are an important part of our national democratic mix. And to keep their place at the top of the pyramid, they appear to be more than prepared to misrepresent and overstate what Conservatives believe and propose. There is little we can do as Conservatives to change them or their counterparts, who are hard-core New Democrats or Bloquistes. They are entitled to their views, and we should always respect their role, but it is our core duty as Conservatives to defeat as many of them as possible in the next election, without, of course, being in any way unkind or less than civil.

What do the words "Prime Minister Harper" really mean? Well, they mean a young, thoughtful, and determined prime minister with integrity and vision.

We all remember how just thirty-six months ago, folks in the country and the media wrote off the coming together of the parties on the centre right in Canada. Well, fresh from winning the leadership of the Alliance, Stephen Harper reached out, and with the able leadership of Progressive Conservative leader Peter MacKay, these two young men did what other good people, including Preston Manning, Stockwell Day, Jean Charest, and Joe Clark, could not. It was not easy. And solid leaders in the national conservative family, like Bill Davis, Ray Speaker, Scott Reid, Loyola Hearn, Don Mazankowski, and Gerry St. Germain, spent an entire summer working on the framework for a new Conservative party, put to referenda in both parties and overwhelmingly passed.

So within weeks of winning the leadership of the Alliance, collaborating with Peter MacKay on creating the Conservative Party, winning a by-election for Parliament, and then winning the leadership of the new Conservative Party, Stephen Harper was thrust into an election called by Prime Minister Martin— an election where many expected the Liberals to win 250 seats and wipe all the opposition parties off the parliamentary map.

Instead, Stephen Harper and our Conservative Party came back to Parliament with the largest Tory opposition since Robert L. Stanfield came within one seat of toppling Mr. Trudeau in 1972, with more seats than both of the old factionalized parties combined. This was a remarkable achievement.

Was the campaign perfect? None are. Did the Conservative Party establish a solid breakthrough in Ontario? Without doubt.

And, last March in Montreal, Conservatives from every region and all walks of life gathered to build a firm policy base that was pragmatic, realistic, and, yes, actually conservative—and in so doing, gave Stephen Harper what he had deserved and earned: a massive vote of party confidence from coast to coast.

Coming back to partisan life after six years at a non-partisan think tank, I believe that good government, sound economic policy, and both our sovereignty and national security would benefit greatly from the election of a Harper Conservative administration.

It is not because I think the Liberals of Paul Martin are corrupt, or venal, or unworthy of governing. As a general principle, we should leave those sorts of attacks to the Bloc or the NDP, or to unhappy parts of the Liberal caucus.

We need a Harper Conservative government because it is high time that the focus in this city and in our national government be on the hard realities and challenges of street-level Canadian life, not the rarefied self-indulgences of the capital city. One criticism I would offer of this Liberal government is that if one put a mirror on every minister's desk, I doubt any would ever go out for lunch. Coming to Ottawa from working elsewhere, one is first knocked over by the level of self-absorption. The notion that the only programs that matter are government programs, the only dollars that count are somebody else's tax dollars sent here for the government to spend, the only real priorities that matter are government priorities—of which this government has cascading, overarching "top" priorities in at least twenty categories—this is essence of self-absorption gone wild.

This is not a government with focus and a central goal. This is a cafeteria of ideas masquerading as a government. It is a cornucopia of goals that add up to no real change, a hit parade of promises that have little follow-up and no real roots in reality. At least the old-time snake-oil salesmen actually had snake oil—this government appears to have only press releases about snake oil, promises about better snake oil, or plans about how to move ahead on the promises to have more press releases about snake oil. And they are so self-absorbed about the process, so self-consumed, that they have forgotten to ask whether any one wants or needs snake oil to begin with.

How would a Harper government differ? First of all, it would leave the snake-oil process to others. It would focus on what really matters to Canadians, like taxpayer rights and fairness, quality modernized and really there health care services, patient rights, and federal and provincial governments that worked together as opposed to at cross-purposes.

A Harper government would ask tough questions about the structure and organization of the federal government, to see where duplication or waste can be reduced, where taxpayer dollars could be more carefully managed, and where efficiency and service levels can be improved. Whenever Liberals find a problem, they reorganize at great cost and with little net benefit to the taxpayer, the level of service, or the hard-working public servant. A Conservative government would embrace a more profound question, and one that all Canadians have the right to ask after all these years of uninterrupted Liberal government: How do we make big government into smart and efficient government—a government that serves the public, as opposed to the other way around?

A Harper Conservative government would respect the core principles of Confederation and not be looking for new ways to spend federal money in provincial jurisdiction while the provinces lack the financial capacity to meet their constitutional duties in areas like health care, education, and welfare.

A Harper Conservative government would not treat Canada-U.S. relations as a public-opinion piñata, to be prodded and pierced to scare up NDP votes and anti-American excess. A Harper Conservative government would make the management of that file an issue of competence and priority. Our leverage in the world has a lot to do with who we are as Canadians, the positions we have taken on global issues, and our strength as an economy; but it also has a lot to do with our relationship as client, customer, and security partner with the United States, and the way we manage that relationship. On this file, despite Ambassador McKenna's outstanding work, we are falling behind. And as a result, the importance of binational institutions like NORAD is very much in doubt. The United States is not the sum total of our foreign-policy priorities—but if we get that relationship wrong, nothing else really matters. A Harper Conservative government would understand that.

We can build the new Conservative Party best by working together with Stephen Harper to build the next Conservative government—a government that will be known for commitments kept, not promises made. *Un gouvernement qui va respecter les priorités confédérales, y compris les revendications légitimes du Québec, et les aspirations de toutes nos provinces. Un gouvernement qui va protéger les minorités linguistiques partout au pays, un gouvernement qui va respecter de façon primordiale nos responsabilités envers l'égalité d'opportunités pour tous nos concitoyens et concitoyennes.*

Nous pouvons construire ce gouvernement, ce gouvernement Harper, si nous restons fidèles au principes de base qui nous ont toujours servis.

We are an inclusive party, and our conservatism is one of equality of opportunity and pluralist diversity. We are a party that believes that what happens around the family table, in classrooms and small businesses, on farms and in church and community halls of all denominations (and no denomination at all) is more important, of greater lasting value and genuine import, than what happens inside any big government. We are a party that stands with the uniformed men and women of our armed services, determined to move heaven and earth so that as they put their lives in danger to protect us, to serve the cause of democracy and humanity worldwide, we give them the support, the training, the advanced kit and assets they need to do the job and safely return home.

We are a party that is determined to address waste and mismanagement in a way that underlines the democratic respect bureaucracies and ministers owe the taxpayers whose hard-earned tax dollars they often spend all too freely.

We are a party that would reach out to the most disadvantaged among us, because Conservatives do not turn their back on those who cannot help themselves through no fault of their own.

The two rules of government that I have always remembered came from two Conservative premiers of Ontario. Mr. Robarts said that ultimately, "good government was the best politics," and William G. Davis said, "Don't put off till tomorrow what you can avoid altogether." Good government does not mean that government needs to be in on every aspect of private life or community aspiration. Good government requires understanding the limits to government. This is not a lesson our Liberal, NDP, or Bloc colleagues will ever understand. It is a message Stephen Harper and Canada's Conservatives are uniquely able to bring to the national table.

Last week, I was sworn in as a member of the Senate of Canada. Now, our upper chamber is venerable, has a constitutional function that is explicit, has done outstanding policy work in areas like health care and defence. But it does not have democratic legitimacy. Conservatives from coast to coast share a belief in democratic reform. We are unhappy that votes are wasted and count for almost nothing in our first-past-the-post system. Prime Minister Martin has said he would not deal with Senate reform unless the provinces first agreed to a plan. Well, I believe that a Harper government could engage the Council of the Federation, established by Premier Charest and encompassing all premiers, in a more activist and focused way on Senate reform in particular and democratic reform in general. And I say to you here this morning, as I said to Stephen Harper on the morning before my appointment was announced, that if a federal-provincial plan emerges where my resignation from the Senate, along with others, would facilitate genuine reform, I would be happy to oblige.

When Prime Minister Martin was gracious enough to appoint me, I indicated that I would not be sitting as an independent or as a Progressive Conservative, despite my respect for those who do. I would be sitting as a Conservative, under the leadership of Stephen Harper, and darn proud to do so.

Stephen has a shadow cabinet that in many respects and personalities outstrips those we actually see on the actual treasury benches in both capacity and judgment. He has helped build a strong Conservative Party that has out-fundraised and out-recruited our Liberal opponents. He has a caucus of men and women representative of the country, and of the face of Canada and the best Canada has to offer.

It is time for Canada to turn the page on a Liberalism that has grown tired, intellectually bankrupt, and devoid of the energy necessary to move Canada forward. It is time to begin a new chapter in our national life—one where community populism and enterprise, prudence and progress, combine with national purpose and respect for the individual to shape our way ahead. It is a conservatism that makes room at the national table for more and more Canadians, that encourages productivity while sustaining our collective commitment to equality of opportunity. Let Liberals and socialists propose the state as guarantor of equality of outcomes, without regard to risk, hard work, skill, and determination. We should plant our flag around the values of opportunity and the ways in which a vibrant economy, neither overtaxed nor overregulated, can make that opportunity real for many more Canadians.

This battle has never mattered more. And Stephen Harper will lead us though it to a resounding victory. All of us should be here to help. It's great to be back in the partisan family I have been part of since Mr. Diefenbaker spoke at my high school in 1962 about the 1961 Bill of Rights his government had passed. Conservatives have a diversity of views, an intensity of debate, and a reflective capacity for the diversity of the country not found among the big-government managerial Liberals. Liberals always ask, "Who will speak for Canada?"—dismissing the provinces, our confederal union, the role of business and labour as they do—because their answer to that self-centred question is always the same: "Who will speak for Canada? Only the Liberals and a bigger and stronger federal government!"

The question Stephen Harper's entire life work has asked is quite different, and it is a question we should recognize as an innately Conservative question. And it is the core question those aspiring to government should always ask: "How can we build a better and stronger Canada?"

That's what Conservatives are about. That is what we have always been about. That is why I am honoured and humbled to be back.

I worried as the 2005–6 campaign began at the end of November that we might still be seduced by the urge to go deeply and personally negative, that there would be reticence to take genuine policy stances, that whoever was doing advertising for the coming campaign did not yet have the capacity to really hit back in the event that the Liberals repeated their successful excess of the 2004 campaign. I worried that beyond a strong focus on accountability and dealing with the Liberal tendency to treat government as "the family business," we would let outrage at Liberal excess become the excuse for a Tory witch hunt, doing what Chrétien and Martin had done themselves. But these worries were groundless.

All in all, I felt substantially better about the hustings this time around than I had at any other time since 1988.

While rumours of my day-to-day presence on the campaign bus or plane were wildly exaggerated, I was involved enough to discern a campaign of immense preparation, strategic underpinning, and policy coherence, for which I give the credit to Harper himself and to the able campaign and shadow cabinet leadership he assembled. This leadership had two tonal underpinnings and one key strategic goal, from what I could judge in the day-to-day campaign connects that his able campaign chair, Doug Findlay, facilitated with a wide range of advisers. The first tonal premise was that a party seeking to govern had to be humble, that voters were to be respected, and that our duty as a party to put substantive evidence of our policy and organizational presence and capacity before the voters whose trust we sought was paramount. Let the Bloc and the Liberals be the ones who took voters for granted—that would not be our stance.

The second tonal premise was not to let the angst over Liberal Adscam corruption invade our own campaign balance. In this regard, the leader's decision to put out the corrective provisions of the accountability package on election financing, tighter fiscal controls, and the like *before* the election was called was inspired. It allowed the party to move on to critical issues like health care waiting times, national defence, and tax cuts without being bogged down by any undue obsession with apparent or real Liberal corruption. A lesson from 2004 had clearly been learned.

Strategically, the "Stand Up for Canada" framework and the "apparent" low-production-value approach to the ads the party launched targeted a voter cohort that Tories had too often left to the other parties, and in this sense it was a remarkable translation of the kind of Canadian that Harper has always seen himself to be. While intellectually rigorous and from a home that was no stranger to the corporate world (his father worked for Imperial Oil), Harper is very much a proxy for middle-income Canadians. Mrs. Harper had her own thriving graphics business in Alberta, and they made the usual sacrifices when the decision to raise a family and put everything into the kids is made, as millions of Canadians profoundly understand. The Harpers and the campaign did not see themselves as part of an Ottawa-based or Toronto-based inner elite always at centre ice, making decisions for their inferiors. Much of Harper's anguish over the Chrétien administration's "culture of entitlement" was a genuine frustration over that administration's sense of its own permanence and its justification by the ongoing Ottawa establishment, honourable or otherwise. So when the campaign rolled out help for parents and for kids' sports equipment, or lower GST rates for everyone, it connected with the "attainable voter" who would normally not take a second look at proponents of ideologically narrow or elite Toryism.

The strategy was clear and precise, well targeted and articulated. The war room was mature and, this time, under the adult supervision of the remarkable Jason Kenney, MP, doing outstanding tactical work during the campaign. The leader was disciplined and focused, and the bus was even-handed and sustained. The media were more than fair, with the able Sandra Buckler managing the outflow from the war room.

And into all this came the imponderables and unpredictables of any campaign—two remarkable events. One was the tragic accidental shooting, in a gang-related event, of an innocent young woman who was going about her Boxing Day sale shopping in downtown Toronto. This immense tragedy opened the population to the traditional Tory get-tough-on-crime message. The other was the decision of the RCMP to confirm in writing to an NDP MP, Judy Wasylycia-Leis, that a preliminary investigation was underway into whether any disclosure or securities laws were broken on the day that the finance minister released the government decision on the taxation of income trusts. The decision to disclose that inquiries were being made long before it had been determined that anything even close to sufficient evidence existed for a charge struck me as extraordinary. It had the effect of moving the spectre of corruption from Chrétien over to the Martin camp. Simply put, it fuelled the "time for a change" subtheme that can so easily threaten any government of long standing. The precedent of the RCMP engaging in this way should trouble everyone, whether it is seen or experienced negatively or positively, however innocent the RCMP's likely intent. For good or ill, it happened, and it helped the Tories immensely.

More importantly, the campaign showed that the Liberals learned very little from 2004. During the close of that campaign, they had succeeded by defining the Tories as hard-right pols with a secret agenda. Now, in the early-2006 election, the Tories—having had a public-policy conference the previous March, running a disciplined campaign without any out-of-line freelancing from candidates, rolling out daily a strong list of policies—had made humility and openness the clear definition of who they were and of the platform they espoused. The Liberal decision to give the Tories thirty days at the outset before serious challenge (assuming that Canadians would not engage till after Christmas) had allowed the Tories to define themselves to the electorate and insulate themselves from desperate late-campaign Liberal attacks, attacks that would come, did come, and, combined with Mr. Harper's well-intentioned musing about the liberal bias of the Supreme Court and the public service, did serve to depress the Tories' seat total—but not enough to keep them out of office or to preserve Martin's political career.

But this was the campaign in which Harper kept the promise of a frank, open, modest, and balanced centre-right Tory platform and campaign. And he delivered big-time, making the Tories not only the government, but a competitive force once again in the battle over the nation's agenda and priorities. Whatever his successes or failures since or in the future, Canadians and Conservatives will owe him their greatest gratitude for this. He had been a catalyst, driver, leader, and inspiration in the long road back.

PART 4

The Road Ahead

17

THE LONG GAME

What are the challenges the Conservative long game must address? To start off, balancing the party's philosophical premises with the tactical and strategic exigencies of day-to-day governance is paramount. Failing to do this would mean political failure. And, in the interests not only of any Conservative but of any democrat who wants a Canadian politics that is open and competitive, Conservatives cannot accept failure as an option.

Another challenge to the party is not to squander its political capital. Now more than ever, the Conservative Party is not a private debating society that wins once in a while and can lose most of the time. The level of taxpayer financial support for all political parties, including the Conservatives, is unprecedented in Canadian history. These funds are expended precisely to keep political parties that garner more than 3 per cent of the federal vote competitive, competent, well run, and able to maintain democratic engagement. That means that competence counts. It counts in policy, in caucus leadership, in parliamentary tactics, in media exposure, and in organizational effectiveness. The Conservative Party's honeymoon is over. The decade of wandering through the wilderness between 1993 and 2003 was not the fault of the Canadian voter, or of Canada's labour, business, or volunteer leadership. It was not the result of something the Liberals, the Bloc Québécois, or the NDP did—they had no duty to help various shades of conservatives sort out their differences. Mulroney, Campbell, Manning, Day, Charest, and Clark all share some aspect of the blame for the lost decade, as do partisans, like myself, who were all too keen to keep the internecine battle going. Mulroney, Manning, Day, and Charest all began working some years ago toward the family's coming together, and even your humble servant began writing in 2000 about what terms of union might look like, but it took the leadership of MacKay and Harper to end the "decade to nowhere" and to rebuild not only one political party but, at the same time, the reality of Canadian democracy.

Relevance always means that the honeymoon is truly over. All the Liberal excesses that were utterly justifiable attack points relative to the elections of 2004 and 2006 have passed into irrelevance.

In philosophical terms, the choice faced by Conservatives can be seen as one of how far right to go on the spectrum only by the naive or myopic. In Canada, the challenge is actually one of establishing a broad economic and social context for change—one where who we are, what we believe in, what we are prepared to protect in terms of core values and essential interests are clearly and precisely laid out.

The challenge is not about committing our military to someone else's foreign policy—be that the policy of the United Nations or of the United States—but how a G8 country can have a rapidly deployable military at home and abroad, allowing us the flexibility to pick our theatres of interest based on our own values, alliances, and challenges.

It is not about the sterile debate between private and public in health care, but about the dimensions of upgrading and modernizing the Canada Health Act and our myriad health-services delivery systems to meet public need and ensure both excellence and accessibility without regard to individual financial net worth. This is about competence and leadership, not ideology.

It is not about simply attacking this program because of waste or that federal program because of misspent dollars. It is about a fundamental rethinking of the financial capacity of different levels of government—all financed by the same burdened taxpayers—and what needs to be done so that those with the greatest legitimate client burdens (the provinces) have the appropriate fiscal capacity to meet those burdens. It is about respecting sections 91 and 92 of the Constitution. It is about protecting francophone minorities right across Canada. It is about electoral and democratic reform so that no more votes are wasted because they do not count in our first-past-the-post, winner-take-all system.

The challenge is also about setting aside the facile attitudes toward Aboriginal peoples and shaping a more inclusive policy that massively expands their uptake in the economic mainstream while ensuring their freedom to maintain their heritage, history, languages, and self-government rights. It is about a vision of the North that links resources to sovereignty and security within a context of fair Aboriginal rights and financial participation. It is about an approach to national security that builds on freedom from fear and the vision of an integrative citizenship and discipline that shapes the dynamic diversity so fundamental to building Canada. It is about an engagement on poverty that, for conservative and societal good reasons, simply will not accept that any Canadian is left behind.

It is about a country that can walk and chew gum at the same time—a country in which we can sort out our domestic priorities without deserting international obligations in our own hemisphere and beyond. A country is more than a hotel whose residents define loyalty in terms of rates, service, and amenities. A country has its own history, values, and cultures, which law-abiding immigrants from all cultures and backgrounds are warmly welcomed to join and embrace. However much new cultures and traditions may shape and enrich our futures, the core Judeo-Christian and consensual values of the Anglo-French and Aboriginal roots of Canada—the roots of tolerance and belief in peace, order, and good government—are *not* open to be redefined in the "whatever seems to accommodate" church of political correctness. The links to our historic and founding principles and institutions are not on the table; they constitute the foundation on which our economic, federal, provincial, and geopolitical choices will always be made. To decouple from monarchist, parliamentary democracy or from our traditional history of standing with our allies would be to decouple from the Canada of Vimy Ridge, Monte Cassino, Juno Beach, the North Atlantic (NATO) charter, the Universal Declaration of Human Rights, the Diefenbaker Bill of Rights, and all that has followed.

And, for Conservatives, reverence for the achievements of the past, caution about trends that are unproven and that are more about novelty than value, need not mean a fear of necessary change. To preserve what is best and repair what no longer works—well, that is a core Tory credo.

Both on the challenges of public policy and on the issue of party coherence and competence, the Conservative mission needs to be one of refining the core goals and strategies that can strengthen the party as a servant of the Canadian public. In opposition, it means planning substantively for both how the party would govern and how, in our democratic processes, we would earn the public trust essential to forming a government. In government, the core task is putting good government and broad public purpose ahead of the siren call of wedge politics and narrow ideology, or the politics of anger, pique, or retribution.

Conservative ideals and principles—about the role of the state, about the importance of the right balance between freedom and responsibility, about the critical juncture between nation and enterprise—need never be a straitjacket limiting perspective or equilibrium. A Conservative government must be in the service of all Canadians, as opposed to only of those who voted Conservative.

Our opportunity is immense. Tactically, the coherence of Conservative government will continue to be welcome to Canadians embittered by the conviction-free Liberal approach. We must seek to grow the brand by adaptive and rigorous policy development. And even more fundamentally, we must understand that our task, as Sun Tzu's *Art of War* suggests, is to separate the Liberals from some of their key constituencies. The core ballot question can be changed and can presage not just one Conservative government term, but many more to come. The question I have suggested become the party's mantra is not the Liberals' "Who will speak for Canada?" but rather, "Who can build a stronger Canada?"

This is the kind of question that means values count—the core values that define Canadians: decency, self-reliance, respect for the law, tolerance, and the responsibilities of citizenship. It is the kind of question that insists that law and order and common responsibilities to each other and to society are the basis of our freedom and of our economic opportunity, the kind of question that allows Conservatives and Canadians to unite the balance between nation and the premises of community, inclusion, and social and environmental justice that the idea of nation implies, and enterprise, with all the motivating forces of freedom, profit, productivity, and expansion it requires. The essence of the mutual dependence between the two is what sets Conservatives, socialists, and Liberals apart. It is an essence that a conservative party worthy of its history and committed to its future should respect and embrace.

It is not the task of the media, the Liberal establishment, the civil service, the judiciary, or the business, labour, or voluntary leadership of the country to help the Tories along the path toward winning their share in the long game. That is the exclusive duty of the Conservative rank and file, the riding and caucus leadership, and the leader.

The challenge is really about shaping a new democratic balance, through regional integration and the electoral will of Canadians themselves. Much has gone well for Canada in the last two decades. In some cases, Liberal and Conservative governments have been part of the problem; in others they have clearly been part of the solution.

The Tory question now is whether Conservatives are committed to actually being part of the political process as contenders as opposed to simply as participants. To be contenders, our vision must be larger than religious sectarianism, wedge politics, or the great luxury of perpetually outraged opposition. Our vision needs to embrace a world of rapid economic change and of new social and demographic developments, an Asia that is rapidly replacing Europe as a key trading and economic focus, and Americas that will face some challenging transitions in the near future.

Our Tory vision must, to do justice to the idea of one national Conservative party, be as large as Canada itself. If alternatives are to be real, Canadians of all persuasions should expect absolutely no less.

A core Tory bias about society is that order and stability are vital to the protection of freedom and opportunity. Without order, there is nothing; with order, when people can go about their daily lives unintimidated and unthreatened, any constructive change is possible.

Tonally, that belief means a government that enforces the law, protects our national security, sustains a strong, national defence, and supports a moderate monetary and fiscal framework. It means not rising to the bait in the House of Commons. It means treating one's reasonable opponents and critics with respect. It means ending the excesses of zealotry—government and history's sweep are greater than any one-act or accountability amendment. It means a PMO that is open, responsive, and disciplined, respectful of the role of ministers and caucus, and too mature and experienced to micromanage. Self-reverence and self-pity are always options, just not good ones.

And as Conservatives, we must let John Diefenbaker's advice—"When hunting big game, do not be distracted by rabbit tracks"—define for us a new and guiding priority. And a Conservative government must go after some big game indeed.

18

The Larger Challenges

In victory or defeat, the approach taken by Stephen Harper and the Conservatives in the early part of the 2005–6 election campaign—connecting the party through ideas for public-policy improvement to a different and improved future—is the right approach. It is an approach that says the core role of a Conservative party is to reflect the values and principles it both cherishes and preserves with practical public policy that either engages the state in or withdraws the state from areas of endeavour where its presence or retraction will advance the public interest.

One of Canada's problems ever since the election of the 1993 Liberal consolidation administration has been an unbecoming focus on itself. This has meant that while hundreds of thousands died of AIDS in sub-Saharan Africa, while parts of the world became substantially unstable, while huge economic shifts took place in India, China, and the Middle East, Canada spent the 1993–2006 period largely looking inward.

That is what can happen when a rising economic tide creates a sense, on the part of a federal government, that it can, with impunity, both arbitrarily cut transfers to the province and subsequently create new federal programs for areas of provincial jurisdiction. And the absence of a coherent national opposition in Canada during that long decade created that kind of licence for federal Liberals—a licence that also allowed the interminable and intensive battle between the Martin and Chrétien factions within their own party.

But the realities of January 23, 2006—the election of the Conservative Party to government—now direct the country and its parliament in a very different way. Consider the following:

- If a new leaf is to be turned, Conservatives in general and Prime Minister Harper in particular must reach out to the other parties in Parliament and to Canadians generally to govern in a consensual way. Any rapid pursuit of a quick Diefenbaker-in-1958-style majority could well produce an unnecessary Clark-in-1980-setback.
- As the Liberals choose a new leader, they will not, as some have suggested, take the heat off the new government in Parliament. Conservatives will have to look to the Bloc and the NDP for substantive support. Fortunately, in Conservative commitments on accountability reform, on beginning a process on fiscal disequilibrium with the provinces, and on electoral reform, there is, if there is the will, ample room for a positive consensual agenda in Parliament.
- The Conservative commitment to accountability will sour with the public if it turns into a witch hunt. Harper was elected as a compelling

new prime minister, not as a chief inquisitor or Crown prosecutor—jobs that are beneath any prime minister, even if they may be necessary aspects of the role of opposition leader.

- The Canada of 2007 and on wants a government that can both ensure that those who stole from the previous government and taxpayers are subjected to the full due process of the law, and that can also turn the page to shape a new beginning. Vengeance is no way to manage a government or inspire a country.

- The 2005–6 campaign was a triumph of Harper's leadership, focus, competence, and team-building skills. It is vital that the high plane achieved in Conservative Party unity not be diminished by the kind of micromanaging that targets rather than inspires, and that red-circles rather than uplifts. Ministers must be given the freedom to be ministers—to hire solid staff and shape their own agendas consistent with government-wide priorities and parliamentary realities. Party voices who were openly counselling between 2004 and 2006 the kind of broad-based, policy-centred mainstream Conservative campaign so expertly led and built by Harper leading up to 2006 should be part of the family. A prime minister must be at the service of the entire party, even those who on occasion have differed with him or her in the past. That is how the Davis and Mulroney and Lougheed and Stanfield leaderships worked so well for so long.

- There needs to be a determined effort to bring some of the better parts of the Alberta Conservative experience—broad caucus involvement in policy development, more cabinet respect for caucus—to the federal Tory experience. An old-style, Pierre Trudeau type of PMO—top-down, interfering with MPs' rights to individual expression—and a cabinet too aloof from caucus colleagues who, except for regional quirks or other nuances could well be in cabinet themselves, would be a serious miscalculation.

- It is one thing to sustain Tory party unity in a pre-election aspirational period (everyone sees a cabinet minister when looking in the mirror), but it is quite another to do so each and every day in government. This remains, always and only, job one. Everything else is secondary to it.
- Non-traditional national interests—young people, Aboriginal people, university and research, science, urban and rural, trade unions, the poor, feminists, and more—must be part of a sincere and substantive outreach mandate. The issue is not what Tories and some of the leadership of these groups may disagree on; it is what common priorities they can agree to and pursue constructively.

For the Conservative government and party, January 23, 2006, was an enormous step ahead. It was the culmination of thirteen years of suffering in the wilderness, of factionalism, egocentric posturing, and political self-regard that created licence for the Liberal Party—to some measurable benefit to aspects of Canadian society, but to some considerable harm as well.

Canadians have tentatively transferred the licence to govern to the Conservative Party. Liberals have been given a time to regroup and rebuild, with 103 MPs and large dollops of public taxpayer support. Conservative breakthroughs in Ontario and Quebec need to be solidified by coherent, steady policy that errs on the side of the inclusive and the humane.

Conservatives will want to seek a new mandate, but they should not rush to do so. They—we—must understand that the public likes minority government, and that the very act of seeking a "majority" as opposed to a "mandate" may diminish the real chance of winning the next election.

And the deliberation by the Canadian public on its next win will be tied very much to the grace, humility, inclusiveness, and balance that Conservatives bring to Ottawa in earnest.

Which, on reflection, is how it should be.

19

The Infrastructure of Civility

In closing this book, allow me a short reflection on the broader Conservative vision.

Conservatives understand symbols and their role in a democratic society, which is why we react with great caution when symbols and what they represent are on the to-change list of the overzealous reformers often to be found in the Liberal Party.

However, as when the flag was replaced in the mid-1960s, a good fight lost against change, however ably advanced, does not mean that the new symbol cannot be embraced. As a teen, I opposed the end of the Red Ensign because I remembered the role of the Crown and the history of British jurisprudence and conventions adapted by Canada and Canadians in the core and basic freedoms Canadians shared. Yet the truth is that

Prime Minister Pearson was right and my boyhood idol, Mr. Diefenbaker, was wrong—wrong for the right reasons, but wrong just the same.

Symbols do matter, and the way a society preserves, protects, and adapts its core premises and symbols is absolutely central to the balance with which it is able to make progress and shape its own future.

In Canada, we have those symbols that are part of our very founding and establishment as a country, that link us to our history and original purpose, and we have newer symbols that reflect the ways in which a modern democracy manages tensions, competing agendas, and sharp-edged aspirations within the context of peace, order, and good government.

For better or for worse, the British North America Act, updated on several occasions by amendment, is the core and basic law of the country. It may not be perfect, but it is fundamental to how laws passed in legislatures and parliaments—whose members we elect or defeat—may operate in this country. The Charter of Rights and Freedoms is part of that act. The political history surrounding this symbol is very clear: we would not have had the original constitution that created Canada unless we had the core guarantees to the provinces, to the separation of powers and responsibilities between Ottawa and the provinces; we would not have had the Charter of Rights and Freedoms in 1982 if we had not had the notwithstanding clause at the same time.

Having been part of the negotiations, on behalf of Ontario's Bill Davis, I can fully certify that when premiers Blakeney and Peckford formally put forward the proposal for a notwithstanding provision, it was so that a province or Ottawa could target a program to a specific group, such as pensioners or young people or Aboriginal Canadians or new immigrants or women, without the Charter being used to quash a provision as "discriminatory." If a program is available to Canadians sixty-five and over, why could someone not petition to have that program extended to people who are only sixty-four, on the basis that the planned program discriminates as to age? The way in which the notwithstanding clause has been typified—as essentially an enemy of equality before the law—is unrealistic, inaccurate, and unjustified. The fear that politicians have about it, either because they have hyped it themselves or because they have been intimidated by others, has had the effect of devaluing the genuine process by which the Charter was born.

In this regard, as I wrote in *No Small Measure: The Conservatives and the Constitution,* co-authored with Nathan Nurgitz, now of the Manitoba Court of the Queen's Bench (then of the Senate), the sorting out of the Charter reflected the balancing of the French Napoleonic-code tradition (where rights are specified and written down) with the British tradition (where citizens have all rights and privileges unless removed by the courts and Parliament). Those who began on the side of parliamentary primacy and who opposed the Charter and its reliance on the courts (the premiers of PEI, Nova Scotia, Newfoundland, Quebec, Manitoba, Saskatchewan, Alberta, BC, and the territories) were prepared to embrace the pro-Charter position of New Brunswick, Ontario, and Ottawa *precisely because* the notwithstanding clause allowed a legislature or Parliament to pass a law or establish a program for up to five years, "notwithstanding the Charter of Rights and Freedoms." That was how the principle of parliamentary supremacy (that is, that the people who elect parliaments and legislatures are sovereign) was preserved. Those who rail against the notwithstanding clause actually rail against that core sovereignty in a democracy.

Tories need to facilitate a broad debate on this issue, in a way that allows the country to reflect on the founding intentions, the choices that have been made, and the balances we need going forward. Whenever a case is made to use the clause, it should always be, as the Constitution provides, a serious matter for wide-open legislative discussion. But it should also be a serious matter when this particular part of the Constitution and the Charter is consigned to the off-limits part of our policy narrative through political posturing that clearly flouts the multi-partisan compromise that patriated the Constitution to begin with.

We also need to take a long hard look at the role of Parliament in the democratic and deliberative part of our governing structure.

The core dynamic and symbolic role of Parliament, as agreed to in the Magna Carta in 1215, was the approval of funds and taxation before the king could spend and tax. The Parliament of Canada has not done this in any effective way since the late 1960s. Essentially, when all parties agreed that program and departmental estimates of spending would be deemed to have been reported back from committee to the House by a certain date, whether they were actually approved or not, that control was lost. There were many arguments at the time in support of this "deemed reported" rule. Too much material for Parliament to consider in the available time was one of them; increasing the length of question period and increasing opposition research budgets to increase *real* parliamentary scrutiny was another—and this in the mid-1970s, when all provincial auditor general acts were changed, along with the federal act, to add "value for money" auditing to the usual audit of probity, parliamentary interest, and integrity. It was argued further that in this way the public interest was strengthened, and the creation of parliamentary officers to join the auditor general, such as the ethics officer, the privacy commissioner, and the freedom of information officer, were seen as further strengthening the public's rights.

None of this is true. And all of it dilutes our parliamentary system and the people's right, through those elected to control the spending of the king.

Runnymede (where the Magna Carta was signed) was not about the right to call expert witnesses after the money has been spent. It was not about the right of committees to have research staff; it was not about the Treasury Board commissioning studies on more efficient administration of the human resources function; it was not about Parliament requiring over one thousand Government of Canada reports from one body or another on financial activities eighteen months ago. It was about approving the king's expenditures *before* they happened and *before* taxes were levied to finance them.

Until we face up to the need to recast Parliament's role so that it can once again perform this task, we are only playing at democracy in a way that actually disenfranchises the voter relative to how his or her tax dollars are spent. Avoiding this principle for more than three decades has led to many core weaknesses in the architecture of democracy in Canada:

- Spending is out of control, if by "control" we in any way mean the prior approval and scrutiny of those elected by Canadians.
- The bureaucracy has been trained and has adapted over the decades to operate largely "notwithstanding Parliament." It is not their fault—they are professionals trying to do their job—but this is a core disconnect between Parliament and the public service.
- This problem is as real in some provinces as in Ottawa.
- Full discussion and debate before expenditure has been replaced by a "retroactive parliamentary posse" (as described by leading academic Denis St. Jacques of Université de Montréal) that passes judgment

many months after the fact, when even 20/20 hindsight is often too late and too biased to be fair or competent. Good programs and honest public servants are unfairly besmirched, along with completely honest recipients of program dollars outside government.

- Parliament and the media are limited to *post factum* individual incidents, which, while often isolated and unrepresentative, occupy huge space in both the activities of the House and its committees, in the media, and in the public's sensibility about government overall. This tends to actually diminish Parliament, government in general, the media, and the conduct of democratic politics. Representatives are attacked, and the public-policy-by-feeding-frenzy cycle dominates.

- Good people are discouraged from either political or public-service stints as part of their life's work.

- The cynicism of this process provides no real guidance to public servants and tends to discourage voter participation, contributing to falling voter turnout.

- Ensuing "freedom of information" and other regimes simply discourage written reports and documentation, making audit-trail activities even more difficult.

In simple terms, the absence of pre-expenditure control gives government a licence that the Magna Carta did not anticipate, and liberates Parliament from anything other than *post factum* posturing, after the horse and the billions are out of the barn.

A process that has been in place to essentially avoid Parliament until well after the dollars are spent (except in the most diluted, pro forma way) cannot be turned around quickly. But at least it must be addressed. The notion that government must proceed with new expenditures whether or not Parliament can come to grips with them needs to be set aside and replaced with a clear rule: No parliamentary approval, no expenditure.

Yes, the timing and priorities of Parliament and committees, the Senate, and the House would have to be altered to make this happen. Parliamentarians who would rather travel to New Zealand to study pro-portional representation may have to spend more time studying and decid-ing on the spending by the chief electoral officer here at home. Yes, going over spending plans and questioning priorities and the rationale behind program priorities may well be tiresome and of less media interest than the scandal-a-day approach to retroactive expenditure control. It is, however, the only way Parliament can have a real role to play in democratic govern-ment between elections. It is the only way the incentives for constructive parliamentary work can progress from the feeding-frenzy retroactivity we now have. Forensic accounting is a hell of a way to set priorities for the future, but the inability of parliamentarians to establish and approve spend-ing priorities before they are out the door is where that cycle will lead.

In terms of both the Constitution and Parliament, this is an agenda around the symbols that are key to the democratic and orderly manage-ment of public business in Canada.

As part of its role in support of Confederation itself, Ottawa must address the fiscal imbalance that sees structural surpluses destroy Ottawa's forecasting credibility while the provinces are awash in fiscal deficits that undermine their capacity to support health care, education, welfare, and other vital areas of primarily provincial jurisdiction.

The infrastructure of civility requires a federal government and Parliament that discharge their democratic role in a way that underlines our values, our history, our innate embrace of pluralism and democracy.

Failure to come to terms with the structural weaknesses in our core approach to balancing the individual's and the state's obligations and rights (the Charter), the citizens' right to democratic parliamentary control of public expenditures, our duties to national defence and security, and some core confederal fiscal sanity can and will likely have explosive consequences. The other road, one of strengthening the expenditure role of Parliament, opening up an inclusive debate on the Charter and the notwithstanding clause, encouraging fiscal cooperation between Ottawa and the provinces, and fully provisioning national defence and security is also available. It is the high road of public-policy coherence for Conservatives, one we should not be afraid to take.

Canada is economically more robust and politically more balanced than at any other time in the last decade. The same may be said of the Conservative Party, and the relative balance and robust circumstance of both is no accident. But anyone who misunderstands the fragility of either misunderstands what we have seen for the last two decades.

In the fiscal disequilibrium challenge, one can find, *in extremis,* the seeds of a unified Quebec position for all parties. The Liberals have not been banished—they have merely been retired to the bench. They will be back, resolute, with new leadership likely detached from the Adscam darkness. And if their leadership can articulate a more balanced vision, Tory victory is by no means assured.

Reaching for a broader view of Canada means reaching out to more Canadians—younger, of colour, First Nations, women, urbane, and urban. It means lifting those down on their luck, in hard straits in rural Canada and in urban economic ghettos, showing that they too are whom we serve.

This is not only about growing the Conservative brand; it is about strengthening Canada and standing up for its future as well as protecting the best of its values and achievements from the past.

And above all, the Conservative brand at its best is modest about what government can do and what politicians should promise; it is at its best humble and self-deprecating.

The road to nowhere—guided by hubris, self-centredness, and ideological politics—was transformed, via humility, to a clear road back. It was humility that helped Harper call MacKay; it was humility that made the policy conference of 2005 in Montreal such a success; it was humility that made 2004 a partial election success; and it was humility that made 2006 the breakthrough that it was.

Humility takes selfless courage and a secure sense of oneself, one's party, and one's mission. That is what the Québécois so enjoyed in the open federalism speech that Harper made last December in Quebec. It was a contrast to the condescension of the Martin Liberals and the presumptive dominance of the Bloc.

The shift from humility to hubris is often the first sign of trouble. With the Liberal party regrouping, with part of the economy overheated, with the NDP and the Bloc needing to shape an election on their terms, with continuing geopolitical instability, there is little reason for hubris—and even less benefit to be derived therefrom.

Humility means needing not only the entire Conservative family, but reaching out to *all* those who share a clear focus on collaborative and humane conservatism, which is about not wedge politics and narrow ideology, but inclusion and opportunity. There is a moderate Conservative consensus that can embrace a range of swing voters and the non-partisan; it can fuel a future Conservative era of values, freedom, progress, and stability; or it can be lost by a perspective too narrow and a bias too partisan. In the end the choice is ours.

Afterword

THE LONG ROAD BACK AND THE ROAD AHEAD

If it seems that Stephen Harper has been Prime Minister of Canada for many years, it is not because so much time has passed, or because his government has gone through controversies of great significance. Rather, it is because the media have subjected him, like most other prime ministers, to daily coverage that has been uniquely intense and corrosive. This coverage is often in excess of actual news value and derives partly from the sheer number of journalists and columnists that Ottawa attracts. Noting that Harper has been prime minister for barely eighteen months may sound defensive but is a simple statement of fact.

Here are some other facts. It has been only thirty-nine months since Stephen Harper won the leadership of a newly created Conservative Party whose members, when they belonged to the various antecedent parties, had been at each other's throats for the preceding seventeen years. And it has been only forty-eight months since representatives of the previously warring factions shaped the basis of the new party, in terms of its form and policy, in the summer and early fall of 2003.

The short lifespans, so far, of the Harper government and the Conservative Party do not excuse whatever may have gone less than right or horribly wrong since the 2006 election. But these factors do suggest a time frame and context that should inform any rational analysis of the challenges that lie ahead. When we reflect on the immediate context of these challenges, let us note that we have seen some remarkable changes in both fortune and tone among the key political actors in Canada. Canada's Liberal Party, still in its own mind the "natural governing party," continues to be obsessed by what it sees as its rude and unjustified removal from its rightful perch. Some Liberals believe this situation would not have occurred were it not for the alleged incompetence, cupidity, craven excess, and narrowness of Paul Martin's coterie. This is wishful thinking of the rankest sort by party factions determined to find blame anywhere but in the mirror. It is surely fair, however, to conclude that prospects would be far more favourable for the Liberals today if the Chrétienites had been more open to an orderly succession; if the victorious Martinites had been more respectful of a prime minister who had delivered three back-to-back majorities for their party; if Ignatieff's supporters had embraced a modest period of apprenticeship for their "Great One"; and if the Rae–Ignatieff forces had been open to some pre–final-ballot collaboration at the Liberal leadership convention in December 2006. One can even imagine a plausible scenario in which the Tories were defeated on their second budget (which did not lack controversial content) and Liberal hegemony was reinstated with a Bob Rae government. Instead, Mr. Harper and the Conservatives continue to face a Liberal Party riven by internal dissent and with a leadership that is more challenged than challenging.

None of this should in any way dilute the prospect (should polls put them substantially ahead in Quebec and Ontario) of the Liberals forming a coalition with any parliamentary ally to defeat the government to try to win back their self-proclaimed birthright. One has only to recall 1979–80 and how easily an electorally defeated and headed-for-retirement Pierre Trudeau—with potential new leaders like John Turner and Donald Macdonald, among others, essentially in the field—was convinced by James Coutts and Keith Davey, and by persuasive poll results from central Canada, to return and retake the government from the hapless Joe Clark. If power abhors a vacuum then for the Liberal Party of Canada potential power, easily regained, subsumes all matters of principle and personal ambition. That's just how Canadian Liberalism works.

But recent shifts in fortune and tone (which have also had their impact on the Bloc Québécois) speak to the range of possible outcomes that Conservatives need to reflect upon as we chart our future path. We Conservatives are not members of a party that easily choose the most practical and successful electoral course. Even the most compelling political pragmatism strikes some more narrow ideologues as demeaning and unprincipled. For some, it is as if the mere prospect of victory or sustained power reflects moral weakness, an unacceptable compromise with the money changers in the temple or the minions of Beelzebub. But the privilege of governing, especially in a pluralist and highly urbanized democracy, is awarded to those who, quite aside from everything else, actually want to govern, with all the compromise and rebalancing the task requires in a pluralist society. Some compromise with other players in a minority parliament is not a sign of weakness. It can be a sign of strength.

Bill Davis regained his majority in Ontario in 1981 because he had largely treated his opposition with respect during the preceding six years when his party governed in a minority situation.

The remarkably short time that has elapsed since the days of two warring Conservative parties, and the broad record of the first eighteen months of Conservative government underscore the finely honed strategic and policy skills of the present prime minister and those closest to him. Every victory has been hard earned for Stephen Harper and his Conservative Party. The real surprise was not that the party did not win a majority in January 2006, considering that it did not even exist in the 2000 election when it was represented by two unpleasantly competitive and divisive forces on the centre right of Canadian politics. The real surprise was that it won at all, given the determined efforts of the small-l and large-L liberal establishment in Ottawa.

The careful balancing, the policies and platform of principle, the mix of candidates that ran as Conservatives in the 2004 and 2006 elections—all of these factors reflect the modernizing role Mr. Harper has assumed and executed so well since winning the leadership. For urban, Maritime, and central Canadian Tories, largely from the Progressive Conservative side of the House, it was essential to embrace the dynamism of the New West, its economic force and political clout. And it was Mr. Harper who provided the leadership to cement a working alliance in that regard, aided by recruits like Jim Flaherty, Tony Clement, Robert Nicholson, and John Baird, and early and courageous partners like Peter MacKay. In the West, Harper's leadership and the roles played by Conservatives like Jim Prentice, Monte Solberg, Chuck Strahl, Vic Toews, and Rona Ambrose revealed a determination to espouse a contemporary conservatism at home and abroad. And the simple, polite, and generous message of "open federalism" in

Quebec—combined with an election campaign that evinced limited but precise policy commitments and competent execution, and treated voters with respect—produced seventeen extra seats in Ontario and a stunning ten-seat addition and breakthrough in Quebec. It was a victory for balance over a monologue of the frantic. The Liberals' panic-driven TV ads, evoking the bogeyman of a secret hard-right agenda by the Conservatives, were too late and too shrill to deny the Tories a victory. Nevertheless, given how cautious Canadians invariably are at election time, these tactics may well have denied the Conservatives a majority.

If there was a particular comparative Liberal lack of balance on campaign and policy execution that helped produce a Conservative victory, what political balance will enable Conservatives to win another mandate to govern in the future?

Assembling the different parts of that balance will not be easy. The challenge is clear: if the Conservative Party only sustains the balance that moved it to power, it may not necessarily be able to broaden its reach to solidify the added seats it took in 2006 in Ontario and its breakthrough seats in Quebec, much less win a majority government.

What, if any, are the structural or political impediments to achieving such a balance? There are several, not all of which are to be found inside the good and the bad of the Conservative Party. Let me start with two: a disengaged and unreformed public service and an apparently loophole-obsessed Department of Finance.

The prime minister has clearly respected the civil service and its existing structure, hierarchy, and internal appointment and patronage systems. The civil service, meanwhile, has yet to fully engage in supporting the Conservative government's program. The bureaucracy might complain, with some justification, that aspects of the government program beyond the initial five-point plan outlined during the election campaign are opaque or non-existent. But that would not justify the apparently narrow advice they have given on income trusts and tax planning, their foot-dragging on new approaches to foreign policy, or their lack of creative advice on other aspects of the Tory platform. Any civil service worth its salt will resist partisan pressure to implement bad policy. In fact, that is part of its statutory duty to the country. But when a party is elected on a broad platform, the Privy Council Office and senior policy leadership in the bureaucracy should seek to offer ways of implementation that are reasonable, affordable, and administratively competent. I voted for the 2007 budget twice and continue to support it despite what appeared to be the hard work of finance and treasury board officials in diluting initiatives for the working poor, or tilting against the middle-class investor.

No new broad balance attempted in a coming Throne Speech or budget will be sustainable unless the government begins the reform of the narrow and often self-serving bureaucracies that dominate Ottawa's upper echelons. On the ground and in the field, federal public servants are working hard, and by and large serving well. This is especially true of our men and women in uniform, at home and in military theatres around the world. But any sense of urgency at policy levels below the frenetic offices of cabinet ministers is, frankly, hard to find. It is not acceptable for the public service to slow policy progress on foreign aid, agriculture, infrastructure, defence, health, and skills development. At some level, the PCO, Treasury Board, and Finance bureaucracies are, if not working against Conservative policy direction, deeply disengaged from its urgency or coherence.

Another impediment is the inability of the PCO, on behalf of the prime minister, to ensure policy coherence. The Court Challenges Program was set aside on the totally reasonable premise that it was not necessary to prime the litigation pump, after a quarter-century of the Charter of Rights and Freedoms and the many court cases over that period. There was general agreement that the litigation option made available by Bill S-3 (passed in November 2005), affording protection to English and French linguistic minorities and enhancing the Official Languages Act, would be provided for in another way. Failure to do anything on this file has needlessly offended francophones, which the prime minister and his ministers had no intention of doing. (In the end, the ministers involved carry the can for this—as they must.) A simple regulatory or programmatic initiative, at minimal cost under existing statutes, could have averted unpleasantness.

The prime minister has been loyal to the idea of a non-partisan public service. Indeed, promotions, both domestic and diplomatic, have overwhelmingly—and almost exclusively—been from within. Expecting and exacting some creativity, energy, and acuity, in return, is not unreasonable.

The second impediment to achieving balance has been the puzzling and excessive zeal among officials in Finance when it comes to closing tax "loopholes." There is apparently a "wait for the Tories' drawer" pathology in that department, which means that pet peeves are emptied onto the desks of new ministers. Finance bureaucrats did this to their minister, John Crosbie, and to Prime Minister Joe Clark in 1979 with the eighteen-cents-a-gallon tax that brought down the government. They did it to Michael Wilson and Prime Minister Mulroney on the GST, which collapsed the Tory poll numbers in the early 1990s to the point that winning an election was impossible (the party's popularity dropped from 29 per cent to 9 per cent in public opinion polls); and they appear to have tried to do the same thing on tax policy to Jim Flaherty and Prime Minister Harper. The political impact of the government's November 2006 decision to tax income trusts is as of yet unclear. The overly imperial Finance Canada has always fought devolution of full mineral royalties to the provinces and territories, and it fights on still—as if it were a political party unto itself.

There is a reason that the Liberals did not embrace a higher gas tax and the GST while in power. Their political instincts told them to let the Tories pay the "political transaction costs" in full before embracing these self-same policies during their next inevitable time in power. Perhaps Finance officials have learned that Tories will pay the transaction costs more readily—"Tory duty" and all that. But we in the Conservative Party must be wary. Such costs are usually steep because the actions that grow out of these policies can run against core Tory voters whose votes can be vital in marginal ridings during the next election.

These two impediments to any Tory rebalancing act need not be fatal. But they set the stage for the early-days angst of a new and minority government, making it difficult for Tories to define and meet all our objectives. But not to worry. A creative Throne Speech containing a firm commitment on Afghanistan and a coherent vision that engages Canadians will quickly settle the nerves of both the governing and the governed.

There are heartening signs in Canada and elsewhere of a new conservatism of substance and balance, one that is secure in its roots and humane in its application. These include the coherent strength of the Conservative government; Prime Minister Harper's clarity of purpose and policy integrity; the hard work of able ministers; the adept adjustment of the government to a more aggressive environmental stance; the open federalism engagement for which most provinces have expressed appreciation; the dilution of the sovereigntist thrust in Quebec; and the serious and focused attention on defence spending and procurement. Moreover, Conservatives have revealed the contours of a Tory policy framework that can and should broaden the party's support base among women, among suburban and urban voters, and among Quebec voters. Elements of this framework include the initial work done to produce a more principled foreign policy, a more robust defence policy, a more sustained interest in helping low-income working Canadians, whether in the cities or on farms, and the streamlining of the Aboriginal land claims process. While there is more to do, solid work has already been achieved on foreign, defence, income security, and tax policy.

What Conservatives can always offer better than others on the political spectrum is a more realistic and pragmatic vision of Canada's geopolitical and economic context. That vision includes forging stronger ties with our hemispheric allies and economic partners; addressing the New Europe and the dynamism of an Asia caught in uneven growth and spurts of wealth and trade; and bringing to health care and to the federal-provincial fiscal and immigration systems the flexibility and adaptation that are needed in twenty-first-century Canada.

These are the kinds of policy thrusts that have characterized Conservatives at their best. As for the present incarnation of the party, the early-days skirmishes over media access, allegedly overly centralized PMO control, message coherence, and enhanced accountability very much mirror what most new minority governments face; the intensity of these skirmishes is to be expected, given the partisan personalities on all sides.

In the end, Stephen Harper's victory over Paul Martin and the end of Liberal hegemony were achieved because Mr. Harper was the leader of a party that most wanted to do a job, and Mr. Martin was the leader of a party that appeared, rightly or wrongly, most eager to keep a job. Canadians showed that they wanted, and still want, a government that gets the job done. From defence to a new hemisphere thrust on foreign and development policy, from courage on Afghanistan (which dare not weaken) to keeping his five initial commitments, Mr. Harper is fulfilling the essential promise of the 2005–06 campaign.

Conservatism is at its best a mix of idealism and realism that tilts away from top-down state initiatives toward the community, the individual, and the collective responsibility of citizens to create and maintain an orderly and free society. Though it may from time to time tilt to the right or the centre, this balance reflects a Canada whose geography and geopolitical role require the skilful interplay of pragmatism and principle. Stephen Harper is the most "Everyman" prime minister we have ever had. His children attend public school. His demeanour, while shy and reserved, is articulate and thoughtful. He is above all a humane and considerate man. Letting more of these qualities show through—for example, by shaping a future vision of northern development and of inclusive economies— would increase his appeal for most Canadians and might well ensure many more years of Conservative government. His visit to Cité Soleil in Haiti was a reflection of the core humanity of his world view.

Keep in mind, however, that the worst exile for Conservatives can be government itself. A party driven by a coherent philosophy of less government, more freedom, lower taxes, and a fiscally restrained bureaucracy is often not comfortable in power. The discomfort and awkwardness that sometimes characterize a new administration are not bad things; at some level they should be reassuring to Canadians. We should fear most the politicians who seem instantly at home with the instruments of government, be they discreet or blunt.

There is a new brand of Conservatism afoot around the globe, reflected in leaders like Angela Merkel, the German chancellor; Nicolas Sarkozy, the president of France; and David Cameron, hopefully a future prime minister of Great Britain. Unlike the rather dour and rigid tones of the waning Bush regime, the governments of these new Conservatives have a practical, conciliatory, and activist bent—one that is optimistic about society and realistic about government. This new Conservative approach is very much Mr. Harper's to shape and define in Canadian terms as his government moves into the latter half of its present term.

How that is done, the extent to which there is idealism and optimism about what Canadian society can achieve—and humility and pragmatism about the relative role of politicians and government—may well determine whether the Conservatives' time in office is a brief interregnum or the first step along a historic new path for Canada and Canadians.

Charleston, Leeds County, Ontario

August 2007

Acknowledgments

I owe a great debt of thanks to, among others, Dr. Kellie Leitch, who read this manuscript through the filter of her role as a youth organizer, party official (national secretary), and campaign chair in a host of federal-provincial efforts with the Conservative Party and the country during the period this effort covers, all while becoming, no less, an orthopaedic paediatric surgeon and assistant dean of medicine at the University of Western Ontario.

As well, my thanks, for his invaluable insights, reflections, and memory, to Graham Fox, who also gave me thoughtful comments on the manuscript, shaped by his remarkable sense as a senior policy adviser for Progressive Conservative leader Jean Charest, as chief of staff to Joe Clark when Clark became leader for the second time (1998), as my senior policy adviser when I ran for leader, and as a key adviser working with my co-chair, Derek Burney, and me on the pre-2004 Tory transition planning group.

Both of these colleagues have clean hands and pure hearts with respect to any miscalculations, factual mistakes, or sins of omission readers may find. Any such mistakes, however inadvertent, are of my own making.

Various other party, public policy, academic, and business luminaries will always have me in their debt. Anna Porter was the first person with whom the idea of this book was discussed. The quality of her advice and encouragement can never be underestimated. There are few reflections on the meaning of contemporary conservatism in Canada that do not benefit from the sagacity and self-deprecating humour and wisdom of William Davis, Ontario's best premier ever and the living anchor for a modern alliance that embodies a deeply rooted conservatism of compassion and sense. Meanwhile, long discussions over the years with Keith Banting, Tom Courchene, Ron Watts, and Tom Kent at Queen's University continue to be a formative force in my own humble efforts at analysis.

Don Bastian, an editor of infinite patience and concurrent acuity, brought focus and precision to initial drafts, as he did to *Beyond Greed* and *In Defence of Civility* some time ago. When an author who is steeped in a subject engages, one often falls into a trap of shorthand, repetitive, and on occasion, obscure and circular prose. I am in debt to Stephanie Fysh, who copy-edited this effort with a deft and creative hand, and to both Anne Holloway and Noelle Zitzer, whose acutely diligent proofreading preserved both author and reader from countless lacunae and oblique sinkholes that, on balance, would have not helped. HarperCollins' Iris Tupholme, to whom we both reported, is an editor-in-chief who can inspire and encourage in ways few could imagine.

To all of these people, and to my executive assistant at the IRPP, Caterina Ciavaglia, who can manage time pressures with the deft hand of an air traffic controller, I owe a large measure of gratitude.

Vicki Rye, my former assistant at Queen's, broke the back of the many drafts of the manuscript, with a capacity to read my longhand as yet unparalleled.

For their forbearance, their challenging and probing questions, and their always independent viewpoints, Donna, my partner in life for over thirty years, and Jacqueline, our daughter and herself a very independent life force, deserve special mention. Each, despite her own compelling career or school pressures, always found the time to test ideas, push back, and challenge any of the intellectual complacency that can, on occasion, infect the most determined analyst.

Kingston, July 2006

Index